CENTRAL ASIA : AN OUTLINE HISTORY

About the Author

Ram Rahul, a native of Delhi, is an eminent scholar of Central Asia. He had his entire education in Delhi. He also studied in the United States of America (USA) in the early 1950s. He retired from Jawaharlal Nahru University as Professor of Central Asian Studies. He also taught the history and politics of South and Central Asia in the USA in 1985-86.

Ram Rahul is the first Indian academic of Central Asia. He has studied Central Asia since 1946. He has also studied Inner Asia, especially Afghanistan and Mongolia. He has travelled extensively on geographical and anthropological expeditions in the Himalaya in the south and Siberia in the north and widely from Korea to Turkey. He has written extensively on Central Asia.

CENTRAL ASIA
AN OUTLINE HISTORY

Ram Rahul

CONCEPT PUBLISHING COMPANY, NEW DELHI 110059

ISBN 81-7022-679-1 (H.B.)
ISBN 81-7022-680-5 (P.B.)

First Published 1997

Published and Printed by
Ashok Kumar Mittal
Concept Publishing Company
A/15-16, Commercial Block, Mohan Garden
New Delhi 110059 (India)

Phones: 5648039, 5649024
Fax: 091–(11)–5598898

Dedication

To Those on Whose Shoulders
I Stand

PREFACE

Central Asia is the central part of the continent of Asia. It has almost two equal eastern and western parts with the Altai-Pamir ranges of mountains as the divide-line from east to west. There have been the movements of peoples and ideas across it. Central Asia has had the proliferation of dynasties, military conquests and empires of Cyrus the Great (559-529 B.C.), Alexander the Great (r. 336-323 B.C.), Chingiz Khan (r. 1205-27) and Timur The Great (r. 1369-1405). Thus it has always been, and is, the crucial part of Asia.

Central Asia, after the advent of imperialism there in the 19th century, has to be studied carefully. The vast documentation leaves no scope for imaginative or speculative research of its history. This documentation, especially since the 1950s, enables an understanding of even the history of the states of contemporary Central Asia, although contemporary has not yet become past there.

Although unique, there is no proper history of Central Asia from the ancient time to the present. The indigenous historical sources of Central Asia are abundant, scanty in no sense. These have not been fully available to research in the world outside. I owe my first awareness of Central Asia to Geoffrey Chaucer (*Canterbury Tales*) and Christopher Marlowe (*Tamburlaine*). Samuel Taylor Coleridge (*Kubla Khan*) also fascinated me as a college student. Lo Chia lun of China and G.N. Roerich of Russia first encouraged me to study Central Asia.

Central Asia : An Outline History is an attempt towards a proper history of Central Asia. I have tried to make it simple and straight forward.

My rendering of the Chinese, Hijri, Russian and Tibetan dates into Gregorian dates is approximate. So also are the Chinese, Russian and other terms and expressions. Excepting explanation of certain terms and expressions, I have dispensed with the generally distracting footnotes, references and other impediments.

Central Asia : An Outline History is not attributable to any specific Source(s) but to general reading and personal experience. It is for beginning students of Central Asia.

Ram Rahul

CONTENTS

Preface 7
1. Setting 11
2. Tibet : Snows and Lamas 22
3. Xinjiang : Dunes and Oases 62
4. Amu-Syr Mesopotamia 97
5. Russo-Soviet Strapy 124
6. Fledgling States 147
Postface 156
Bibliography 158
Index 160

1

SETTING

Central Asia is the centre of the continent of Asia between Mongolia and China proper in the east, India, Bhutan, Nepal and Afghanistan in the south, Iran and the Caspian Sea in the west and the Ural range of mountains and Russia in the north. It consists of almost two equal parts—East Central Asia (Tibet and Xinjiang) and West Central Asia (Kazakstan, Kirgizstan, Tajikistan, Uzbekistan and Turkmenistan).

There are several concepts of Central Asia, especially the Chinese, Indian and Iranian concepts. The Chinese concept comprehends it as Hsi Yu, the land west of China proper. China was the first country to appear in East Central Asia in the time of the first Han dynasty. And Balkh, although politically part of Afghanistan, is geographically part of West Central Asia. According to the Indian concept, Central Asia is the land north of the Himalaya* and Hindukush mountains. Ladakh, although it is politically part of India, is geographically part of East Central Asia. And Balkh, although it is politically part of Afghanistan, is geographically part of West Central Asia. According to the Iranian concept, it is the land north of Khurasan. With the advance of Russia eastwards in the seventeenth century, there also has been the Russian, and Western concept of Central Asia as the land east of the Caspian Sea.

There are several dimensions and aspects of Central Asia. Geography and anthropology are its most important dimensions and imperialism is its

---

* *Hima* + *alaya*, "Abode of snow", that is the land of snow.

most important aspect. The terrain, climate and flora and fauna have affected the lifestyles and cultures within it: nomadism and sedentarism. There is no comprehensive study of the geography and anthropology of Central Asia. Such a study is necessary for the proper study of this land of unique configuration—high mountains, large rivers, big deserts and fertile oases and the homeland of diverse peoples. Except Mongol imperialism, there is no direct study or critique of imperialism, whether Persian (Cyrus the Great) and Greek (Alexander the Great) in ancient times and Russian/Soviet and Japanese in modern times, in Central Asia. Until recently, political borders in Central Asia changed with the shifts in political power there.

Tibet is an ancient land of ancient people. Now it is the autonomous region of the People's Republic of China (PRC). It marches along the autonomous region of Xinjiang of the PRC in the north and China proper in the east. It touches Myanmar/Burma and borders India, Bhutan and Nepal in the south and west. Most of it is a plateau. Tsaidam is the lowest part of this plateau. The Tibetans also spread in Myanmar/Burma and in Yunnan, Sichuan (Szechwan) and Gansu (Kansu) in China proper. The ancient Chinese knew it as *T'u-fan*. The ancient Indians knew it as *Bhota**. Owing to the presence of gold in its Changthang (*Byang* thang) highland, the ancient Greeks called it the land of "gold-digging ants". The Arabs called it *Tubot* (*Tubot* is Arabic for *mTo bod,* Upper Tibet). The name *Tibet* drives from *Tubot.*

Bon Chhos, the cult of nature and magic, was the faith of the people of ancient Tibet. Mount Tise and Lake Mapham** are the most sacred places of the

---

* Bhota is the Sanskrit variant of Bod, Tibet. The modified form of *Bod* is *Po.* Hence Bodpa Popa, the people of Tibet.

** Kailash and Manas Sarovar of the Sanskrit tradition.

Bonpos, the adherents of the Bon faith. The Bonpos go around them from right to left. They always keep sacred objects on their left side. The symbols of Bon such as the Yung dKrung* can still be seen in Lamayuru, Ladakh (La dvaks). The *Gonpa,* the *Vihara/* Monastery, of Lamayuru was originally a Bonpo building. The domain of Bon in ancient times was Shang Shung (later Guge) in West Tibet. Bon is still a living faith in Tibet and its borderlands. Of course the ancient history of the eastern borderlands of Tibet is obscure. The present Bon codex, institutions and practices bear the deep impact of the Buddhism of Tibet. The geographical names in Tibet such as Comolungmo (Mount Everest) on the Nepal-Tibet border and Chomolhari on the Bhutan-Tibet border are mostly from the ancient Bon period.

In modern times, Tibet has been called "the land of the lamas" because of their dominance of its life and politics. They had established themselves as its rulers by the middle of the thirteenth century when, in 1260, Kubilai Khan (Qubilai Qan, 1216-94) of China gave the governance of Tibet to Lama Lodo Gyaltshen Phaka (bLa ma Phags pa, 1235-74), the then head of the Sakya (Sa skya) Sect of the Buddhism of Tibet.

The sources of the great rivers of Asia—the Huang He(Ho) and Yangze (Yangtse) of China and Tsangpo/ Brahmaputra and Sindhu (Indus) of India, which flow into the Pacific and Indian Oceans - lie in Tibet. The Tsangpo is the greatest of Tibet's waterways. Like the Sanskrit word *Ganga,* the Tibetan word *Tsangpo* (*gTsang* po) means "river". And, like the Ganga, the Tsangpo means this particular river. The Tsang Chhu, the river of Tsang, is its main tributary. The word *Chhu* is Tibetan for "river", "water".

---

* The right to left Svastika (Su+asti+ka).

The human habitation in Tibet is generally at a height of ten thousand feet above the level of the sea. If at some places it is at lower levels, at others it is as high as fourteen thousand feet. By reason of such height, it experiences severe cold, and its hills and valleys are almost devoid of vegetation. The struggle for existence in Tibet in ancient times thus was great. And, in search of a remedy, the people of ancient Tibet restricted the growth of their population by having one wife for all brothers in a family. The adoption of polyandry partly obviated the difficulties and for generations the same house and the same plot of land sufficed without any need for extension.

Xinjiang (Sinkiang) is an ancient land. It borders Mongolia and the PRC province of Qinghai (Ch'inghai) in the east. It marches along Tibet and India in the south, it straddles Afghanistan and Tajikistan in the west and it is adjacent to Russia, Kazakstan and Kirgizstan in the north. The name *Sinkiang* (Chinese : New Territory) is only from 1768 A.D., when the Manchu Ch'ing government of China merged Kashgaria, south of the Tianshan (T'ienshan) range, and Zungaria, north of it, to form it. It made Sinkiang a province of China on 14 November 1884.

In the ancient time, the Chinese knew the entire land west of Ch'ang-an, the capital of the then China, as Hsi Yu, the Western Region. The Mongol Chagatai period knew it as Mogolistan. Since then, it has been the eastern part of what the Moroccan traveller Ibn Battuta (1304-68) called it *Turkistan,* the land inhabited by the Turks. In the modern period, it has been known both as *Alti Shahr,* the six cities of Kashgarh, Yarkand, Khotan, Aksu, Kucha and Turpan (Turfan; Chin:T'u-lu-fan). Since 1955, it has been the Xinjiang Uigur Autonomous Region (XUAR) of the People's Republic of China. It has been called the "heart", the "pulse", the "pivot" of Asia.

The Tianshan, the Celestial Mountain range, divides Xinjiang into two distinct, northern and southern, parts. The southern part is bigger than the northern part. The northern part is mainly pasture land. Urumqi (Urumch'i), the capital, is in the northern part. The Chinese call it Hungmiaotsu, which is the translation of the Mongol word Urumch'i. Kashgarh, Yarkand and Khotan and the other cities are in the southern part. The Turpan Depression and Taklamakan Desert are also in the southern part. The Chinese expression *liu sha,* "moving sand", most aptly describes the Taklamakan Desert. The Tarim River is the life-giver/lifeline of the southern part.

The Ili River in the northern part and the Tarim River in the southern part are the main rivers of Xinjiang. The Ili River, the joint waters of the Kunges, Tekkes and Yulduz rivers, which rise in the Tianshan range flows north into Lake Balkash, the largest lake of Central Asia, in Kazakstan. The Tarim River, the joint waters of the Yarkand, Khotan, Charchan and other rivers, which rise in the Karakoram and Kunlun (pronounced Kuenlun) mountains, flows east across the Gobi Desert into Lake Lob Nor. The Manas River in the northern part is Xinjiang's deepest river. It is the granary of North Xinjiang.

The people of different ethnic and linguistic origins such as the Han, Uigur, Kirgiz (Kirkiz), Kazak, Mongol, Manchu, Tajik, Balti and others live in Xinjiang. The Uigurs are the most numerous, and constitute nearly half of its population. The Hans (population almost equal to the Uigur population) have been in the Tarim Basin for much longer than the Uigurs. They are, in a way, the indigenous people of Xinjiang. They mainly live in the cities. The Huis/Dungans (Tungans), Kazaks and others came to Xinjiang in the mid-eighteenth century. The people of Indian origin lived in the oasis kingdoms up to the advent of the Uigurs from the Orkhon region of present-day Mongolia in the ninth century A.D. The scholar pilgrims Fa Hsian (337-422), Hsuan Tsang (596\602-664) and others to India in the fifth-seventh centuries mention them; they mention their kings, their religion—Buddhism — and their *viharas*/monasteries. They also mention their Sanṣkrit language and scripts.

West Central Asia extends from Iran and the Caspian Sea in the west to the Tianshan range and China in the east and from Siberia in the north to Afghanistan in the south. What is West Central Asia now was Bukhara once, and what was Bukhara once is West Central Asia now.

Bukhara* is an ancient land. The tribes of ancient Central Asia nomadized on this antique land. Before Islam, Zoroastrism and Buddhism prospered there. It was the stomping ground of Alexander (356-323 B.C.) of Macedon. Bukhara became the capital of the Saman dynasty (892-999) founded by Isma'il Saman (b. 849). Although Persian, in its Tajiki form, continues to be spoken by people in the cities of ancient Bukhara even today, the Saman dynasty was the last Persian dynasty to rule Central Asia. After 999 and after the Turkization of West Central Asia, Bukhara became the cultural capital of Turkistan.

The glory of Bukhara resounds in folklore and poetry. Its history and culture are fascinating indeed. It emerged as an important city of Central Asia in the late fifth and early six centuries A.D., and as the centre of Islamic learning and theology by the end of the tenth century. Except for the holy places connected with Prophet Muhammad, Bukhara has been the nucleus of the Sunni philosophy. The name Bukhara derives from *vihara*, the site of a Zoroastrian temple.

---

* Bukhara is from Pahlavi/Sanskrit *Vihara*, "Temple".

Turkmenistan is an ancient land. Alexander took in 329-327 BC what is the Turkmen region now. The Parthian kingdom (200 BC-AD 10) of the 3rd century BC, south-east of the Caspian Sea, thrived on its territory. They built their capital at Nisa, and a flourishing civilization. Marv (pronounced Merv, modern Mari) in Khurasan was a great centre on the Silk Road in the ancient time. Islam first came to Marv in 651 AD. Present-day Turkmenistan extends from Uzbekistan in the north to Iran in the south and from Afghanistan in the east to the Caspian Sea in the west. The Turkmens spread in Afghanistan, Iran, Kazakstan and Uzbekistan. They are not the indigenous people of Turkmenistan : they are the descendants of the Uigurs. The term *Turkmen* first appears in Islamic sources in the 10th century. The Turkmen language is now the most standard of all the Turki languages of the Eastern and Western Turks.

Tajikistan is an ancient land of an ancient people. It borders on Uzbekistan, Afghanistan, Kirgizstan and China. The Tajiks of Iranian origin are the most ancient people of West Central Asia. They were the first people in Central Asia to convert to Islam. They are adherents of both the Sunni and Shii sects of Islam. They first adhered to the fire and light religion of Zoroaster (Zarathustra). Even now there are vestiges of the folk culture of Zoroasterism among the Ismaili/Moulai Tajiks of the Pamir mountains. The Tajiks in the Pamir region, called *Galchas,* are purest of the people of Iranian stock. The Tajiks spread in Afghanistan, Uzbekistan and Xinjiang (China).

The Kirgizes are an ancient people. The Kirgizes of the Yenisei River basin in Siberia destroyed the Uigur empire (744-840) centred at Kara Balgasun on the upper reaches of the Onon River in present-day Mongolia. The Uigurs moved westwards. The Kirgizes call their land *Altyn Beshik,* "Golden Homeland", situated between the Alatau and Tianshan ranges. Kirgizstan borders on China in the east, Tajikistan in the south and Kazakstan and Uzbekistan in the north and west. The Kirgizes also spread in Kazakstan, Uzbekistan Tajikistan and Xinjiang (China).

The Uzbeks of the Dasht-i Kipchak, the Kipchak Steppe* north-east of the Caspian Sea, were the last nomad conquerors of West Central Asia. They emerged in West Central Asia towards the end of the fifteenth century. They were of mixed Mongol and Turk origin. They had been converted to Islam, its Sunni Sect, before emerging in Central Asia. Khvarazm (pronounced Khorezm) was the last to fall to them in the seventeenth century.

The Uzbeks, who took to the agrarian and village way of life, are the *Sarts* of the Russian annals. The Uzbeks, who continued their nomadic way of life, became known as the *Kipchak*. The Kipchaks, nomadic Uzbeks, of Namangan in Farghana (pronounced Ferhaana) and the Kirgizes are close to each other. The Kipchaks adopted the Kirgiz way of life. Like the other tribes north and west of the Caspian Sea, the Uzbeks first appear in the history of West Central Asia in the fourteenth-fifteenth centuries. They were nomads then. After arriving in the lands between the Amu Darya and Syr Darya in the sixteenth century, they became agriculturists in the oases.

The Kazaks do not appear in Central Asia before the sixteenth century. Muhammad Hayder Duglat, the author of the *Tarikh-i Rashidi,* was the first to mention them in the Uzbek context. He also mentioned the name Kazak separately. He called the Kirgiz *Kirakir.* Before the territorial delimitation of West Central Asia in 1924, the Russians, and

* *Dasht-i Kipchak* of the Muhammadan sources and *Zolotaya Orda,* "Golden Horde" of the Russian annals.

Westerners called the Kazaks *Kirgizes* and the Kirgizes *Kara Kirgizes*. The names *Kazak* and *Uzbek* were originally political, not ethnical.

Up to the Mongol invasion of Central Asia in 1220, there also were other equally great centres there such as Khorezm (modern Khiva) on the left bank of the lower Amu Darya and Marv, of course not of the grandeur and glory of Bukhara. Until the delimitation commission of 1924, West Central Asia consisted of two parts : (1) Russian/Soviet Turkistan and (2) Uzbek Khanates.

West Central Asia has high mountains, big glaciers, great lakes and big rivers and great deserts. Its highest peaks are in the Pamir region—*bam-e dunia*. "roof of the world". They have been named and renamed several times. The Soviet period knew them as Lenin, Communism and Chaika (Seagull, named after the call sign of the first woman cosmonaut). The big rivers (that is, the Amu Darya and Syr Darya) rise in the Pamir and Tianshan ranges in the east and flow into the Aral Sea in the north. The ancient Greeks and Romans called them Oxus and Jaxartes. The Arabs called them Sayhun and Jayhun. The Panj and Vaksh make up the Amu Darya. The Zarafshan River rises in the Western Pamir range and disappears in the Kizilkum Desert. The Chu (River) rises in the Tianshan range and disappears in the steppes of Kazakstan. The great lakes are Issik Kul in Kirgizstan and Balkash in Kazakstan. Issik Kul, situated in a fold of the Tianshan, is a vast inland sea. (*Kul* is Turki for lake). The Kirgizes built their first settlement there after their arrival from Siberia in the ninth century. The Naryn River, the upper reaches of the *Syr* Darya, is the largest river of Kirgizstan. The great deserts, the Karakum in Turkmenistan and Kizilkum in Kazakstan, are also there.

Central Asia has always been, and is, the crucial part of Asia, and an important region of the world. It has been the crossroads of civilizations, the battleground of armies and the proliferation of dynasties. In the ancient time, Buddhism and Islam spread from Central Asia to East Asia. Buddhism made a lasting impact on the cultures of China and Korea and Japan. In the medieval time, science (mathematics, astronomy) spread from Central Asia to West Asia and Europe. Temujin (1167-1227), the great Khan of the Mongols, united Central Asia into one sovereignty. The Mongols ruled China, Persia (traditional name of Iran) and Russia, and menaced India. The Turks almost but not quite repeated the performance. China escaped conquest by them : Emir Timur (1336-1405) of Samarkand* died in the northern frontier town of Otrar in the winter of 1405 on his way to conquer it. But the Turks conquered India : Zahiruddin Muhammad Babar (1483-1530) founded an empire, the Moghul empire, in India in 1526. Later, strong neighbours prevented the peoples of Central Asia from expanding outwards. The ancient Silk Road (the term has been in vogue since the nineteenth century) from China to Europe through Central Asia had become obsolete. Portugal had established the sea route between Europe and India and China in the fifteenth century.

In modern times, China and Russia possessed Central Asia equally, China its eastern part (that is, Tibet and Xinjiang) and Russia its western part (that is, Kazakstan, Kirgizstan, Tajikiztan, Uzbekistan and Turkmenistan). For a time, from the 1960s to the 1980s, they also contested for supremacy there. Russia withdrew from its part of Central Asia in the middle of 1991. China continues to hold its part. And, if

* *kand* is Persian for “city”, “town”.

history can be an illustration, it will continue to do so.

Britain based in India and Japan based in China also involved themselves in Central Asia. On 12 August 1905, Britain and Japan even made an alliance against Russia in Asia. The British awareness of Central Asia traced to its position in Persia in the eighteenth century. The Japanese awareness of Central Asia traced to Shogun Toyotomi Hideyoshi (1537-98), who after unifying the island-empire of Japan in 1590, led a military expedition to Pyongyang, Korea, to conquer China in 1592. The Chinese drove him into the Sea of Japan.

In 1991, a part of Central Asia, that is Western Central Asia, emerged politically, but it is still undeveloped academically. It has generally been studied in the context of China, India and Iran (and Russia in the context of modern Central Asia) and from the outside inward. It has not been studied in its own context. For the proper understanding of Central Asia, it must be studied in its own context. *Central Asia : An Outline History* is an attempt to do this. This foreground sets the framework.

2

TIBET : SNOWS AND LAMAS

The early history of Tibet, an ancient land of an ancient people, is obscure. There are no annals or chronicles of pre-history Tibet. It had no system of writing then, although, according to the lamas of its ancient faith—Bon, Tibet had a system of writing. According to the historical sources of ancient China, the Ch'iang* tribes of the Tibetan stock of Lake Kokonor harried its northern frontiers up to the 3rd century A.D.

Tibet emerged in history with Songtsen Gampo** (Srong brtsan sgam po, reign 618-49 AD) of the Yarlung (Yar klungs) Valley of Kongpo (rKong po) who succeeded his father *Tsanpo*** (bTsan po*) Namri Songtsen (gNam ri Srong brtsan, *crica* r. AD 570-618) as its first king at the age of 13. Namri Songtsen consolidated the tribes of Tibet. Songtsen Gampo might not have been the first king to unite them, but he certainly was its first historical king. Nyathi Tsenpo

---

* Like all the non-Han people of ancient China, the Ch'iang tribesmen were the allies of the Hsiung-nus in the time of Matun (r. 209-124 BC). As the later day Tangut (Chinese : Ho-hsi, Hsi-hsi) of Gansu (Kansu), they were also allies of the Liao state and maintained diplomatic relation with it. They created their own empire in the region of East Kokonor in 982, which Chingiz Khan destroyed in 1227. The royal house of the erstwhile princely state of Sikkim claimed descent from the Tanguts as the Minyaks of Amdo.

** The suffix *Gampo* denotes "high power", po being the ending suffix as in Balpo (ancient Nepal), Kongpo, Sogpo (Mongols), Tsangpo, et cetera.

*** Chief, King

(gNya' khri brtsan po), is the first king of Tibet, according to the Bon tradition. He had descended from heaven. According to the Buddhist tradition of Tibet, he had gone from India to Tibet in the late 2nd century B.C. via the Kur Chhu, the upper reaches of the Manas River of Bhutan, which rises in Tibet. According to the folk legends, he built the first castle Yumbu Lakhar in the Yarlung Valley

Yarlung Monarchy

Tsanpo Songtsen Gampo organized his tribesmen and made out of them strong warriors, with whose help he subjugated adjacent U (dbUs) and Tsang (gTsang), the central region of Tibet. His horsemen galloped from Bhutan* in the south to Gilgit (Tibetan : Bru sha) in the west. He destroyed even the state of the Ch'iang tribes. Kongpo remained semi-autonomous.

Tsanpo Songtsen introduced many measures in Tibet. He transferred his capital from the Yarlung Valley to the bank of the Kyi (sKyid) Chhu, a northern tributary of the Tsangpo. And what was *Rasa,* the place of the goats, became *Lhasa,* the place of the gods. He built there a castle, the Potala. Later, the Potala became the site of the palace of the Dalai Lama. Songtsen proclaimed *Lha Chhos dGe ba bChu*(Ten Religious Principles) and the *Mi chhos gTsang* ma bChu drug* (Sixteen Principles of Human Conduct), Tibet's first ethical and legal codes.

King Songtsen married Princess Bhrikuti Devi (Tib : Belsa) of Nepal. He married Princess Wen-ch'eng (Tib : Gyasa) of China, the daughter of Emperor T'ai-tsung (r. 629-49), the son of Kao-tsu (r. 618-27), the founder of the T'ang dynasty of China (618-907). He had also married a Ch'iang/ Tangut princess. Bhrikuti Devi took with her the images of Akshobhya, Maitreya and Tara. To enshrine them, King Songtsen built the Jo Khang.**

* *Bhota+anta,* end of Tibet.

** Popularly known as the temple of Chho Rinpochhe.

It faced south towards India. The Jo Khang is the most holy place in Tibet. More than thirteen centuries have gone by since its construction, but it is still as fresh a structure as though it had been constructed only recently. Wen-ch'eng brought with her a sandalwood image of the Buddha, which had gone from India to China via Khotan (North-East Central Asia). To enshrine it. King Songtsen constructed the Ramochhe (Ra mo chhe) in the north of Lhasa. It faced east towards China. It is still extant. The sandalwood image of the Buddha had been transferred from the Ramochhe to the Jo Khang after his death.

The chief Tibetan wife, Mongza Thichham Nyandongteng (Mong bza' Khri lchham mnyan dong steng) of King Songtsen bore him the heir, Gungsong. Songtsen also had by his Nepalese wife a son who had died during his lifetime.

King Songtsen had able ministers, Gar Tongtsen (mGar sTong brtsan) and Thonmi (Thon mi)* among others. Gar (d. 664) also served as envoy to Nepal to escort Princess Bhrikuti Devi to Lhasa. Songtsen also sent him to China to receive Princess Wen-ch'eng. Gar also acted as regent to King Mangsong Mangtsen (r. 650-76), the grandson of Songtsen Gampo. His sons played great roles in building the Tibetan empire.

King Songtsen sent Thonmi* of Village Thon, and others to Kashmir to study Sanskrit and devise an alphabet for the Tibetan language. On return from India, Thonmi devised the Tibetan alphabet on the model of the alphabet of contemporary North India. He dropped some of the Indian letters as the Tibetan language had no need of them. For some of the sounds

*Thonmi is known as Sambhota (*Sam+Bhota*), the Good Tibetan, in India.

peculiar to the Tibetan language, he made separate letters adding a stroke on some letters, thus forming *ts, tsh, z* and *dz*, including *a* as a consonant, *et cetera*. He also wrote the grammar of the Tibetan language. He was thus the first grammarian of Tibet. His grammatical treatise is still standard work.

According to tradition, Songtsen and Thonmi together translated, in the script devised by the latter, several Sanskrit works. Only a few of those translations survive now. The first translation of Sanskrit works into Tibetan thus began in the time of King Songtsen.

Songtsen Gampo accepted Buddhism, which, helped by the efforts of missionaries from India, such as Acharyas Shantirakshita (Tib : Shiba tsho, d. 797) of the Nalanda Vihara, Atisha Deepankara Srijnana (983-1054) of the Vikramasila Vihara of Magadha (India) and others had a deep impact on the subsequent destiny of Tibet. King Songtsen and the Tibetan nobility thus came in contact with the civilizations of India and China. Acceptance of Buddhism and creation of the alphabet for the Tibetan language were the greatest accomplish-ments of King Songtsen. Buddhism opened a vision for developing Tibet from a primitive to a civilized country. Buddhism had reached China, via Khotan, by 56 AD (and Korea by 372 and Japan by 538). But it did not reach Tibet, India's geographical neighbour, till the 640s, the reason being the people of Tibet still in the tribal stage.

King Songtsen thus brought Tibet to the notice of history not only by imperial, but also by pious deeds. On his death in Phanyul in 649, his kingdom comprised the upper Huang He (Ho)* region in the north, the upper Himalaya region in the south and the Pamir region in the west.

**He (Ho)* is Chinese for "river".

Mangsong Mangtsen (Mang srong Mang btsan, r. 649-67), the grandson of Songtsen, succeeded him. Although, before the great majesty of his grandfather, the valour of Tsanpo Mangsong Mangtsen paled, yet he defeated the forces of Emperor Kao-tsung (r. 649-83) when the latter tried to recover the territories which his grandfather had taken from China.

Thisong Mangje (Khri srong Mang rje, r. 676-704), the son of Tsanpo Mangsong Mangtsen, married Princess Wun Sin-kong, a daughter of Emperor Kao-tsung. He died in 704, during a campaign in the Mo-so kingdom (Tib : 'Jeng) in the later-day Yunnan of China. Thide Tsug (Khri lde gTsug), the infant son of Thisong Mangje, ascended the throne. Finding an infant on the throne of Tibet, China tried to recover its territories from Tibet. Emperor Chung-tsung (r. 705-10) gave his daughter Chin-ch'eng (Tib : Kim sheng) in marriage to Tsanpo Thide Tsugten (r. 704-55) in 710. She died in 739. Thide Tsugten also married a Mo-so princess, Ma Thitsun, who bore him a heir, Lhabon (Lhas bon). Lhabon died before Thide Tungten.

Thisong Detsen (Khri srong 1de btsan, b. 742; r. 756-97), born near Samye (bSam yas) in Kongpo, south-east of Lhasa, succeeded his father Thide Tsugten. With the resumption of the struggle with China over Liyul/Khotan, the forces of Tibet held it. They also took most of what now are China's Gansu and Sichuan provinces and parts of North Yunnan. They captured Ch'ang-an (now Xian in Shaanxi), the capital of T'ang China, in 762, and set up Guang-bu, a prince, on the throne. The Emperor had fled. Dunhuang (Tun-huang), the frontier town in the heart of the Gobi Desert and near the western terminus of the Great Wall of China, fell to Tibet in 781and remained in its possession up to 848. The Uigurs helped the Chinese against the

Tibetans. In order to terminate the constant conflict, which had gone on since the first year of Emperor Su-tsung (r. 756-62), China and Tibet concluded their first bilingual treaty in the reign of Emperor Te-tsung (r. 779-804) at Ch'ing-shui in Gansu in early 783.

Whenever there is a change of faith in a country, certain characteristics and values of the old faith become a part of the new faith. This is what happened in Tibet as well. Buddhism in Tibet accepted certain deities and modes of worship of the Bon Chhos, the Bon faith. There, however, was a struggle between Bon and Buddhism for supremacy. While some nobles of Tibet did not like the foreign religion, Buddhism, and preferred their old faith Bon, others were enthusiastic about it. King Thisong Detsen wanted to propagate Buddhism in Tibet. He invited Acharya Shantirakshita of the Nalanda Vihara (Magadha), India. Following this event, there were portents of certain natural calamities in the country. The protagonists of Bon said that the gods of Tibet, enraged at the introduction of Buddhism, were punishing the people with these visitations. King Thisong sent Acharya Shantirakshita to Samye.

Buddhism had come to Tibet two centuries ago. But neither had any Buddhist monastery been built there nor had any Tibetan been ordained as a Buddhist monk. According to the direction of Acharya Shantirakshita, King Thisong Detsen founded the first Buddhist *gonpa*/vihara/monastery at Samye on the model of Udantapuri Vihara, founded by King Dharmapala (760-815) of the Paladynasty (750-1060) in Magadha in 786. When the construction of the Samye Monastery was proceeding, Acharya Shantirakshita sent for twelve monks from Nalanda for the ordination of Tibetan monks, perhaps as a precaution, for the rules laid down a quorum of five monks for the purpose. They ordained the first seven Tibetans—Yas shis dbang po, Gtsang dpal byangs, Rma Rin chhen mchhog, Tshul khrim dbang po srung pa, Khon klu dbang po of Sakya, Lha'i dbang po srung pa and Pagor Vairochana. Rinchhenchhog emerged as one of the first *lotsaba,* translators from Sanskrit into Tibetan. The Tibetans call Shantirakshita *mKhanchhen Bodhisattva.* His *Tattva Sangraha* manifests his profound scholarship.

After the death of Acharya Shantirakshita at Samye of a kick from a horse in 997, Chinese monks (perhaps from Khotan) in Tibet created some trouble. Thereon King Thisong invited Kamalasheela, the chief disciple of Acharya Shantirakshita, from Nalanda. The legendary Padmasambhava, also of Nalanda, contended with the guardians of the Bon faith. His place in the pantheon of Tibetan Buddhism is next to that of the Buddha himself. Tibetans reverently call him *Guru Rinpochhe,* "Precious Teacher". Kamalasheela averted the crisis. In 792, King Thisong held the philosophical debate between the monks Hashang of China (perhaps of Khotan) and Kamalasheela at the Samye Monastery to determine the right method of attaining enlightenment. The Indian view—the gradual progress—triumphed over the Chinese view—the instant progress. Hashang acceded to the Indian view by garlanding Kamalasheela. King Thisong had proclaimed Buddism as the state religion of Tibet in 779. He had made his wife, Queen Ye shes mtsho rgyal, the head of religious affairs for her steadfast faith in the teaching of the Buddha. She had venerated and honoured the panditas and lotsabas.

Muthi Tsenpo (sMu khri bTsan po, r. 797-804), who succeeded his father Thisong Detsen (-he had abdicated), had been brought up in an atmosphere charged with the Bodhisattva ideal—renunciation of one's own salvation for removing the suffering of others.

In persuit of this ideal, he endeavoured to remove economic inequality among his people by the equal distribution of wealth. He did not perhaps realize that the equal distribution of wealth without the equal distribution of work was not the right solution. His experiments, which encouraged idleness on the one hand and resentment on the other, frightened the nobility, including his mother Tshepongza Magyal donkar (Tshe spong bza rMa rgyal ldon skar) of the Bon nobility. She herself had placed him on the throne.

Thide Songtsen or Senalek (r. 804-815) succeeded his younger brother Muthi Tsenpo. Before his time, Tibetan translations from other languages had been carried on haphazardly. He introduced the method of translation (still unexcelled) to preserve at least eighty per cent of the equivalents of the original vocabularies in an ingenous way. These works, compiled in 814, have been known as *Mahavyutpatti(s)* and had been included in the *Tangyur* (*bsTan gyur*). The system of having definite words for all roots, prefixes and suffixes, which thus evolved, has been found to bc invaluable for the purpose of the restoration of the original texts.

Thitsug Detsen (also known as Repachan, r. 816-36), the youngest son of Muthi Tsenpo, succeeded him, superseding his elder brother Darma. Emperor Mu-tsung (r. 821-25) of China thought of an alliance with Thitsug Detsen. The Uigur Turks of Karabalgasun-on-Orkhon River, who were then threatening the Tibetan position in Khotan/Liyul, influenced the rapprochement between China and Tibet, which concluded a treaty, based on parity, at Ch'ang-an in 821-22. Eventually, the alliance between China and the Uigurs led to Tibet's withdrawal from Khotan. The Uigurs had helped the T'ang rulers to suppress the rebellion of General An Lu-shan during the reign of

Emperor Su-tsung (756-62). The power of the T'ang dynasty was on the decline in 842.

Repachan (Ral pa chan) had the events of his reign recorded chronologically. He also introduced in the country a system of weights and measures from India. He venerated the Buddhist monkhood. Darma, the superseded prince, took the opportunity to spread all sorts of rumour against Repachan and his monks, including the rumour that Ben Chhenpo Dangka Pekyi Yonten (Bran ka dPal kyi yon), the Buddhist monk chief minister of Repachan, had intimate relations with Queen Nantshulma. Repachan sentenced them to death. Owing to the slur on her honour, Nantshulma committed suicide. Ben Chhenpo fled north, ultimately caught and executed.The Bon conspirators killed Repachan in the garden/of the Shampa palace, east of Lhasa, in 836.

After the assassination of Repachan, Darma (r. 836-42), nicknamed Glang Darma, Darma the Bull, by Tibetan Buddhists because of his bull-like size, ascended the throne. He outlawed Buddhism. He rewarded Wegyal (dB's rgyal), the assassin of Repachan, by appointing him chief minister. He started to persecute the Buddhists in 841. He closed down not only the Buddhist monasteries, but even Tsuglag Khang and removed the image of the Buddha from the Jo Khang. He ordered the Buddhist monks to marry and take to secular life. He even banished, from Lhasa, his eldest brother Tsema (bTsad ma). Prince Tsema established a principality in the then East Bhutan. Several ancient Bhutanese clans claimed descent from him. According to the tradition of Tibetan Buddhism, the persecution of Buddhists failed. Buddhist monks, who had escaped to Kham, East Tibet, and had taken the Buddhist texts with them, returned to Central Tibet and revived Buddhism there.

They renovated the old Buddhist monasteries, and established new ones. The custom of sticking out one's tongue allegedly started in the time of King Darma.

The Yarlung Monarchy (AD 618-842) had maintained its realm with vigour for about 225 years, though powerful Chinese and Muslim realms surrounded it—a distinction which scarcely fell to the lot of any other country in the world then. It had active diplomatic relations with the kingdom of Dali (Ta-li) (in the modern province of Yunnan, China) in the east and Sogd in the west. It collapsed due to internecine feuding. Its social, political and economic structure was feudal. There was constant rivalry among the noble factions at the court. The *rGyal rabs gsal ba'i me long*, Clear Mirror of Royal Genealogy, of bSo nams rGyal mtshan (1312-75) of Sakya covers the period of the Yarlung Monarchy.

The Yarlung Monarchy continued for a couple of generations, but it was beyond the power of Osung and Yumten, the sons of King Darma, to restore the Songtsen line to its former glory. Osung, the son of the Junior Queen Tshepong Za, possessed the western part and Yumten, the son of the Senior Queen sNanam Za, possessed the eastern part. The descendants of Osung and Yumten left Lhasa, and moved westwards and eastwards.

From the collapse of the monarchy of the Songtsen line in the 840s to the establishment of the theocracy of the Buddhism of the Sakya Sect of Sakya (Sa skya) in the 1260s, there was no unified central authority, no state in Tibet : no single government ruled Tibet. And there were frequent disturbances in the country.

Tashi Tsen, the king of Purang (sPu 'rang) in Ngari (mNga'ris), called Prince Kyide Nyimagon (sKyid lde Nyi ma mgon, 900-30), the second son of Khortsen, to his capital Taglakhar and offered his only daughter

Doza Khorchong ('Bro bza 'Khor skyong) in marriage to him, and also nominated him his successor. Kyide Nyimagon thus became the lord of Ngari Korsum (mNga' ris bskor gsum, that is, Purang, Guge (Gu dge) and Gartok) and of the adjacent countries of Ladakh (La daks) and Spiti (Spi ti). He gave his kingdom to his three sons Pelgyigon, Tashigon and Detsugon. Detsugon (1De gtsug mgon) received Guge (Gu ge). Mangde, the eldest son, succeeded him, became a Buddhist monk and took the name of Yeshi Od (Ye shes 'Od).

Guge Monarchy

Yeshi Od founded the Tholing yonpa (Thod gling dGonpa), the first Buddhist monastery in Western Tibet. His descendants have been known as the priest-kings of Guge. The Kingdom of Guge, formerly Shang Shung, flourished up to 1679 when Dalai Lama Lobzang Gyatso (1617-82) declared war against Ladakh. It dominated even Spiti. Antonio d' Andrada, the Portuguese Jesuit from Goa, who visited Tsaparang, the capital of the Kingdom of Guge, via Garhwal, in 1624, mentioned it in his travel account. He visited Guge several times between 1624 and 1641.

Yeshi Od perceived the degeneration of Buddhism, the only monument of his ancestors. He sent Rinchhen Zangpo (958-1055), the abbot of the Tholing Gonpa, and other boys to Kashmir around 975 to study Buddhism there. Kashmir being a hot place for people from Tibet, out of them only Rinchhen Zangpo and Legpa Sherab returned alive. Rinchhen Zangpo built many monasteries and temples in Guge, Ladakh and Spiti, several of them still extant. The frescoes in the Alchi temples in Ladakh and the Tabo temple in Spiti by artists from Kashmir are excellent specimens of the Indian art of the 8th-10th centuries. Rinchhen

Zangpo performed the funeral rites of King Yeshi Od. He also associated himself with Acharya Atisha Deepankara Srijnana, who went to Guge in 1042.

Yeshi Od then invited Acharya Atisha Deepankara Srijnana, shortly Atisha (982-1054), of the Vikramasila Vihara in Magadha, India. Atisha was not able to accept his invitation then. According to the tradition of Tibetan Buddhism, Yeshi Od again resolved to send for a teacher from India. In order to collect the amount of gold required for the purpose, he went to the Changthang mountains. There the men of the Karluk Turk tribe of Yarkand captured him. Prince Changchhub Od (Byang chhub 'od) went to Yarkand to obtain the release of King Yeshi Od. The Khan of Yarkand demanded heavy ransom. Before going to fetch the required amount, Prince Changchhub went to see Yeshi Od in prison.

Yeshi Od said to Prince Changchhub not to waste the gold, saying : "You know that I am already an old man. Even if I do not die now, I shall not live more than ten years. If you give away this gold, you will not be able to bring a teacher from India, and to reform Buddhism. How well it will be, if you will leave me to die here in the cause of Chhos*, and, by sending that gold to India, bring a teacher. Besides, what reliance can you put on this king, that even after getting the required amount of ransom, he will release me? So, my son, do not trouble about me, but send men to India to bring Atisha. This time, when he will think of the cause and of my imprisonment, for its sake he will surely do us the favour of visiting our country. If he is not able to come, then bring some other teacher from among those under him". So saying, King Yeshi blessed Prince Changchhub by placing his hands upon his head. This incident became the theme

* *Chhos* is Tibetan for Dharma.

of a secular drama in Western Tibet.

Changchhub entrusted Gungthangpa, Nag tsho Tsbul khrims, who had once before been to India, to bring Acharya Atisha. The touching resolution of King Yeshi moved Atisha. On the proper occasion he informed Sthavira Ratnakarapada (Ratnakarashanta), the head of Vihara Sangha. It was difficult for Ratnakarapada to consent to Atisha to leave Vikramasila in the circumstances of the time. Any way, when Atisha reached Tsaparang, the capital of Guge, via Nepal, King Changchhub received him royally. From West Tibet, Atisha moved eastwards to Central Tibet, dying at Narthang in 1054. Since then the Kagyur and Tangyur wooden printing blocks have been at Narthang.

Atisha restored Buddhist monastic discipline in Tibet. He translated Sanskrit works into Tibetan with the help of lotsawas and revised such works as had been translated before him. This was the second spread of Buddhism in Tibet, the first spread being in the time of King Songtsen Gampo. The original works of Atisha, including his *Bodhipathapradeepa*, are available no longer, but their translations have been preserved in the *Tangyur*, Domton ('Brom ston, 1005-64), the pupil and successor of Atisha, wrote the life of his teacher.

The passing of Atisha marked the end of the period of ancient Tibet. Tibetan Buddhism of the pre-Atisha period has since been known as the rNyingmag/ Old Tradition and that of the post-Atisha period as the Sarma/New Tradition. All the sects of the New Tradition, that is the Sakya (Sa skya), Kargyut (bKa brgyud) and Gelug (dGe lugs) respect Atisha equally.

Marpa (1012-99) founded the Kragyut (White) Sect. He had studied under Naropa (d. 1038), one of the 84 *siddhas* of India. Milarepa (Mi la ras pa, 1052-1123) of the Kagyu Sect was the greatest *siddha* (*dubthob*) of Tibet. His parents had been adherents of the Nyingmapa Sect. Lobzang Dakpa (bLo bzang Grags pa, 1357-1419) of Village Tsongkha (Amdo, North-East Tibet) founded the Gelug (Yellow) Sect in the beginning of the fifteenth century. The Gelug Sect even traces its origin to Atisha. Tsongkhapa was among the spiritual descendants of Gyalwai Domton. The Kadam (bKa gdams) Sect of Atisha merged into the Gelug Sect. So the Gelug Sect is also known as the New Kadam Sect. While the other schools of the New Tradition lay emphasis on learning and meditation, the Gelug school lays emphasis on learning and austerity.

With the end of the translation activity from Sanskrit into Tibetan, from the middle of the 7th century to the middle of the 13th, Buton Rinchhen Dub (Bu ston Rin chhen Grub, 1290-1364), the great monk scholar, collected all the translated works into *Kagyur* (bKa' 'gyur) and *Tangyur* (bsTan 'gyur) after systematizing them. Very few works have been added to the two collections after the 13th century.

Regency of Mongol China

The theocratic governance of Tibet began, when Kublai Khan (Qubilai Qan; Chinese : Shi tsu, b. 1215, r. 1260-95) and the second son of Tolui Khan (r. 1229-41), the younger brother of Mongu Khan (r. 1251-59) and a grandson of Chingiz Khan (Chinggis Qan, 1167-1227), became Khan of China in 1259. He created the state of the Sakya (Grey) Sect and made Lama Lodo Gyaltshen Phakpa (1235-80) the vicegerent of the Mongols in Tibet in 1260. Lama Phakpa, the nephew of the Sakya Pandita, Kunga Gyaltshen (1182-1251), thus was the first religious hierarch to rule Tibet. Of course, theocracy as an institution was only from 1271.

Kublai Khan designated Lama Lodo Gyaltshen Phakpa *Kuo-shih*, the National Preceptor, and *Ti-shih*, the Imperial Preceptor, in 1270. He himself embraced

Buddhism and made the Buddhism of the Sakya Sect the official religion of the Central Asian part of Mongol China. This placed Tibet and China on the *mchhod yon*, spiritual-temporal relationship, implying the supre- macy of the superior of the Sakya Sect of Buddhism of Tibet over the emperor of China. Lama Phakpa devised a square script, called the Phakpa script, based on the Tibetan alphabet, for the Mongol language in 1269.

Kublai Khan authorized supervision of the regency at Sakya by lay *Ponchhen*, administrators, holding the charge of civil affairs in *Chokha gsum**. Grumpa Shakya Zangpo (d. 1275), the first Ponchhen, organized Tibet in *Khri skor Chu gsum*, "Thirteen Districts", each *thikor* consisting of ten thousand homesteads administered by a lay man. The system excluded the Sakya domain and the appanages of the Mongol princes** in Central Tibet. Sakya continued as a principality up to 1951, when the People's Republic of China (PRC) overwhelmed Tibet. The Sakya theocracy was short. The Sakyapa succession was from uncle to nephew. The medieval period of Tibet had started with the Sakya rule of the country.The *Deb ther dmar po*/Red Annals, compiled in 1346, also covers the Sakya period (1271-1342).

The grand lamas of the other sects, especially the Brigung subsect of the Kagyud Sect, emerged supreme in the secular politics of Tibet in the fourteenth century. Prince Changchhub Gyaltshen (1302-73) of the Phagmodubpa family of Nedong, one of the *thikor chusum* in the Tsangpo Valley, overthrew the Sakya regime in 1350. He changed the administrative system of Tibet, when he assumed its control in 1354, establishing the Dzong (fortress) in place of the *thikor* system.

---

* U, Tsang and Ngari, i.e., Central, South and West Tibet.

** Including the Mongol princes of the Ilkhan dynasty (1256-1335/54) of Mongol Persia.

The Phagdu rule in Tibet was simultaneous with the Ming dynasty (1368-1644) of China. Except for Tibet's frontier regions such as Kham bordering China, and adjusting relations with other border regions, the Ming rulers did not take much interest in Tibet. Of course, the Emperor Wan Li (r. 1573-1620) invited Dalai Lama Yonten Gyatso (1588-1617) of the Gelug Sect to Peking in 1615. He had also invited Dalai Lama Sonam Gyatso (1543-88), the second rebirth of Lama Gedun Dub (1391-1475), in 1583. To gain Ming patronage prominent lamas of the different sects and secular manor lords of Tibet went to Peking all the time. The benevolence of the Ming emperors bestowed on them consigments of silk, tea, etc. Tibet resumed the *ula* (Chin : Yishan) system in its regions bordering China.

The Dalai Lama line had traced to Lama Gedun Dub, the principal disciple of Lama Tsongkhapa, who had founded the Gelug Sect to reform Tibetan Buddhism. Lama Sonam Gyatso had been the teacher of Phagmodu Dakpa Jungne, an adherent of the Kagyu Sect. Dakpa Jungne supported Lama Sonam Gyatso to extend the work of his predecessors. When Dakpa Jungne passed away in 1564, the royal family requested Lama Sonam Gyatso to perform the funeral rites.

Lama Sonam Gyatso took Buddhism to Altan Khan (r. 1543-83), the Khan of all Mongols, and his Tumet Mongols of the Ordos-Suiyuan region on 19 June 1578. Altan Khan praised Sonam Gyatso for his wide range (Dalai) knowledge, conferring the title "Dalai blama rDo rje Chhang" on Lama Sonam Gyatso and Lama Sonam Gyatso conferring the title "Chhos kyi rgyal po", the Righteous King, on Altan Khan. The Gelug dignitaries applied the title retrospectively to Lamas Gedun Dub and Gedun Gyatso, the first and the second grand lamas of the Gelug Sect. This created the institution of the Dalai Lama.

Supported by the Tshurphu Monastery, Donyo Dorji of Rinpung (East Tsang), the minister of Phagmodu and relative of the Phagmodu royal family by marriage, seized power in 1481. Ngawang Jigdak, the last Rinpungpa ruler, was a man of letters who translated several works from Sanskrit into Tibetan. The people nicknamed him *Gyalpo Pandita*, the *Royal* Scholar. Concerning Ngawang Jigdak as Gyalpo Pandita, there is an interesting anecdote. When he was losing the battle to Tsheten Dorji, his own governor of Samdubtse (later Shigatse, West Tsang), his wife mentioned this to him. He said to her that it did not matter, for he had composed his poem.

Tsheten Dorji (r. 1618-22) rebelled against the Rinpungpa and seized power in 1618, taking the title *Depa Tsangpa*, the King of Tsang, the title later changing to *Desi Tsangpa*. The Desi Tsangpas patronized the Karmapa, a subsect of the Kagyud School, and suppressed the Gelug Sect.

Gushi Khan (Tib : Tenzin Chhokyi Gyalpo, 1582-1655) of the Khoshot Mongol tribe of the Horyul, the Kokonor region, marched into Amdo and Kham in 1635 and into U-Tsang in 1641. He defeated Desi Karma Tenchong (r. 1622-42), and put him to death, in 1642. Excepting certain minor local kings, Karma Tenchong was the last secular ruler of Tibet. Gushi Khan had already, in 1639, defeated and executed the king of Ber, the adherent of Bon, in Kham, and ally of Karma Tenchong. Gushi Khan, who patronized the Gelug Sect, offered Tibet to Dalai Lama V, Lobzang Gyatso (1617-82), and proclaimed himself *Gyalpo*/ King of Tibet. This is how the Gelugpas acquired the political power in Tibet. The theocratic system of governance in Tibet thus further consolidated. Gushi Khan had moved, along with his retainers, from the Ili River Valley to Kokonor in the 1630s.

Initially, the lay and religious potentates of Tibet resisted the authority of Dalai Lama Lobzang Gyatso. But, when he acted as one who belonged to all the traditions of the country, including Bon, they acknowledged him as the supreme pontiff of the country. The emergence of the Dalai Lama as the head of Tibet ended the sectarian and secular schisms in the country.

Gelug Theocracy

Dalai Lama Lobzang Gyatso organized his government on the principle *Chhosi Shungdel*, the government of religion and politics, that is, the system of governance in which both monks and laymen take part. The integration of religion and politics strengthened even the social status of the theocratic system of governance in Tibet. Dalai Lama Lobzang Gyatso also declared Lhasa, founded by King Songtsen Gampo, to be the divine seat and the political capital of Tibet. Lhasa eventually became the cultural and commercial capital as well even though Shigatse and other old centres retained their importance.

When Emperor Shun Chih (1636-61)*, who had transferred from Mukden to Peking,** began to reign in 1650, the Manchu court invited Dalai Lama Lobzang Gyatso. The Dalai Lama went to Peking in 1652. The Manchu court had also invited Panchhen Lama Chhokyi Lobzang Gyaltsen (1567-1687), who had declined the invitation on account of his old age.

The boy emperor welcomed the Dalai Lama warmly and with reverence. He had Buddhist upbringing. His mother Empress Dowager Bumbutai was a

---

* 9th son of Abahai (1592-1643), 8th son of Nurhachi (1559-1626).

** Ming China had fallen to the Manchus in 1644.

Buddhist Mongol princess. And so were his two wives and three concubines. Hence his reverence for the Dalai Lama. There are anecdotes that Emperor Shun Chih ended his life as a Buddhist monk.

Emperor Shun Chih conferred great honours on Dalai Lama Lobzang Gyatso, specially the title "Vajradhara Dalai Lama". The Dalai Lama gave Emperor Shun Chih the title "Gnam gyi lha'jams dbyangs gong ma bdag po chhen po". This equation between the Manchu Emperor and the Dalai Lama established the *mchhod yon*, the donor donee, relationship between them. The high Gelug lamas had thought the Manchu Emperor to be the incarnation of Manjushri Bodhisattva.

The officials of Tibet were in the habit of wearing a variety of costumes. On return from China, Dalai Lama Lobzang Gyatso decreed that they wear the court dress of ancient Tibet. The war against Ladakh of Gyalpo Delek Namgyal (r. 1666-95) in 1679 was one of the last acts of Dalai Lama Lobzang Gyatso. This eventually involved Tibet with Mughal India, then suzerain of Ladakh. A Mughal army from Kashmir and Kabul under Fidai Khan, the son of Ibrahim Khan (Mughal governor of Kashmir), chased the Mongol-Tibetan army from Basgo to Lake Panggong Tso in 1682. Lama Mipham Wangpo of the Dukpa Kagyu, as the plenipotentiary of Dalai Lama Lobzang Gyatso to Gyalpo Delek Namgyal, settled the terms ceding Ngari, except Village Mensar near Mount Kailash and Lake Manassarovar to Tibet. The peace treaty of 1683 fixed the Ladakh-Tibet border at the Lhari Chhu near Demchok and regulated trade relations between Ladakh and Tibet.

Dalai Lama Lobzang Gyatso was not entirely free from the stipulations of the *mchhod yon* relationship. The Manchu court did not like his conferring the title "Boshugtu" (Blessed), in 1678 on Galdan Khan (r. 1676-97) of the Oirat Mongols of the Ili Valley, the rival of the Manchus then. The Dalai Lama does not then seem to have been friendly to the Manchu regime. The alliance of his Desi Sanggye Gyatso with Galdan Khan led to complications for Tibet in the early 1700s.

Dalai Lama Lobzang Gyatso wrote extensively. He wrote not only his own autobiography but also the biographies of the Third and Fourth Dalai Lamas. He wrote the biography of the Fourth Dalai Lamas, Yonten Gyatso, during his journey to Peking in 1652. He knew Sanskrit and cultivated it. He encouraged Tibetans to study in India. The last translation from Sanskrit into Tibetan seems to have been made in his time in 1665. The modern period of Tibet started, in a way, in his time.

Tsangyang Gyatso (1683-1706), the rebirth of Dalai Lama Lobzang Gyatso enthroned in 1696, was an unusual Dalai Lama. Lobzang Khan, the Mongol king of Tibet since 1703 and the great grandson of Gushi Khan, criticized the living style of Tsangyang Gyatso. Tsangyang Gyatso composed and sang fine songs. The themes of his songs are autobiographical .

Lobzang Khan declared Tsangyang Gyatso a fraud and replaced him by Yeshi Gyatso of the Chakpori Medical College on the edge of Lhasa as the true rebirth of Dalai Lama Lobzang Gyatso. He had Tsangyang Gyatso taken to the Mongol camp at Lhalu near Lhasa. Although Tsangyang Gyatso exercised no bearing on the politics of the day, this negated neither the importance nor the prestige of the Dalai Lama as an institution. The Tibetans, who considered even the living style of Tsangyang Gyatso to be the test of their faith in the Dalai Lama, strongly resented the treatment meted out to him by Lobzang Khan. They resisted his deposition of Tsangyang Gyatso. The lamas of the Depung Monastery, along with those of Sera, attacked the party taking him to the Mongol camp, and guarded him.

Lobzang Khan killed Desi Sangge Gyatso in 1705 and contrived the murder of Dalai Lama Tsangyang Gyatso in Kokonor in 1706. The Tibetans looked for help to Chhewang Araptan (r. 1697-1727), the ruler of the Mongols of the Ili Valley and the nephew of Galdan Khan (1632-97). An expedition commanded by Chhewang Dondub, the cousin of Chhewang Araptan, took Lhasa on 30 November—1 December 1717. Lobzang Khan died while escaping northwards. The Zungars imprisoned his Dalai Lama, Yeshi Gyatso. Thus ended the influence of the Khoshot Mongols in Tibet.

The elimination of Lobzang Khan was most disquieting to Emperor K'ang Hsi (r. 1662-1722), the second emperor of Manchu China and the third son of Emperor Shun Chih. With a remarkable volte-face, K'ang Hsi put himself as the champion of legitimacy. After keeping Kesang Gyatso (1708-57), the rebirth of Dalai Lama Tsangyang Gyatso, under surveillance at the Kumbum Monastery in Amdo for nearly ten years, he recognized him (Kesang Gyatso) as the seventh Dalai Lama. A Manchu detachment, commanded by. General Yen Hsi and escorting Kesang Gyatso from Kumbum to Lhasa, entered Lhasa on 24 September 1720 and drove the Zungars out of Tibet. It installed Kesang Gyatso on the throne in the Potala on 16 October 1720. This was the first instance of troops from China ever entering Lhasa. From then until the fall of the Manchu dynasty in 1912, the Manchu Ch'ing government stationed an Amban, a Manchu mandarin, and a military escort in Tibet.

The arrangement of 1720 did not work well. And the court of Yung Ch'eng (r. 1722-35), the third emperor of Manchu China, appointed its first Amban at Lhasa. It removed both Dalai Lama Kesang Gyatso and his father Sonam Dargye from Lhasa to their native Village Garthar in Lithang, and Derge (sDe dge), in 1728 for seven years. This was so because the Dalai Lama had proved to be the rallying-point for certain Tibetans, who sparked off a civil strife in 1727. Sonam Tobgye Phola, who was victorious in the civil strife, had suspected the Dalai Lama to be under the influence of his councillors Ngapho Dorji Gyalpo of Kongpo, Lumpa Tashi Gyalpo of Tsang and Jarawa Lodo Gyalpo with Sonam Gyalpo Khangchhen as their head. Their execution on 1 November 1727 led to the rise of his (Phola's) power.

Phola also intervened in the civil strife in Bhutan in 1730. His intervention resulted in the establishment of the supremacy of Tibet over Bhutan. The Bhutanese government stationed a representative as ransom at Lhasa. Later, this enabled the Manchu Ch'ing government to claim suzerainty over Bhutan, etc.

Protectorate of Manchu China

Prince Gyurmi Namgyal, the younger son and successor of Phola on the latter's death on 12 March 1747, wanted to end the Manchu influence in Tibet. Ambans Fuch'ing and Labdon sensing trouble invited him to their *yamen* (office) ostensibly for a conference on 11 November 1750, and then assassinated him. The supporters of Gyurmi Namgyal such as Lobzang Tashi managed to incite an anti-Manchu riot in Lhasa and besieged and burnt the Chinese yamen. They killed Labdon and many of the civilian staff as well as the escort. Fuch'ing committed suicide on 11 November 1750. Ch'ien Lung (r. 1736-96, d. 1799), the fourth son of Emperor Yung Cheng and the fourth emperor of Manchu China, appointed General Bandi (d. 1755), who had promulgated orders of Emperor K'ang Hsi about the zoning of areas in Tibet, Sichuan and Yunnan in 1725, in their place and sent a military force to Lhasa from Sichuan to restore Manchu authority. The Manchu court made four Tibetans of equal rank in charge of civil affairs, placing Dalai Lama Kesang Gyatso at the apex. For Dalai Lama Kesang Gyatso, although he had devoted his entire time to meditation, had remained the crucial factor in the politics of the day. The Manchus pretended that they were just to help keep up the situation in Tibet as at the time of Dalai Lama Lobzang Gyatso.

Bhutan had intervened in the struggle for succession in Koch Bihar. The claimant had sought the help of the government of the English East India Company (Calcutta). The government of the Company, which was keen to expand towards the Himalaya, drove out the Bhutanese soldiers. Panchhen Lama Lobzang Palden Yeshi (1737-80) interceded with Warren Hastings, first Governor General of Fort William (Calcutta) from 1774 to 1785, on behalf of Bhutan, which had been under the suzerainty of Tibet since the 1730s. Dalai Lama Jampel Gyatso (1759-1804) was minor then. Warren Hastings, availing himself of the intercession of the Panchhen Lama, sent George Bogle to him via Bhutan to open trade relations between India and Tibet. Bogle was the first Englishman to visit Tibet. Wumi T'ai, the Manchu Amban in Tibet from 1773 to 1775, and the Regent of Tibet refused to permit Bogle to visit Lhasa. Bogle cultivated a close intimacy with the family of the Panchhen Lama. He even married a Tibetan lady, described as a sister of Panchhen lama Lobzang Palden Yeshi. Warren Hastings also sent Captain Samuel Turner to Shigatse, also via Bhutan, in 1783. The government of Tibet also refused his request to visit Lhasa.

Tibet's relations with Nepal (Ne+pala) deteriorated owing to its help to Sikkim (Sukhim)* in the latter's difficulties with Nepal in the 1770s. So much so that Nepal invaded Tibet in 1788. On learning of Nepal's request for military help from the government of the East India Company in the Nepal-Tibet conflict, Dalai Lama Jampel Gyatso wrote to Lord Charles Cornwallis, the Governor-General of Fort William (Calcutta) from 1786 to 1793, to desist from assisting Nepal. He was the first Dalai ever to address a communication to the British government in India.

The Nepal-Tibet conflict traced to the first half of the seventeenth century when the Kingdom of Kathmandu circulated its pure silver coins in Tibet. This was beneficial to Kathmandu, because Tibet paid for those coins in gold or provided the silver required for their minting from which Kathmandu deducted a certain percentage of silver. Later, Kathmandu sent debased coins to Lhasa.

After Prithvinarayan Shah of the Kingdom of Gorkha (r. 1742-68) had conquered the Malla kingdoms of the Nepal Valley, Kathmandu and Lhasa tried to solve the coinage issue. But before its solution, another problem, which had worsened relations between Tibet and Nepal, was Tibet's help to Sikkim during its war with Nepal in 1779. Yet another problem further complicated the situation between Nepal and Tibet. On the death of Panchhen Lama Lobzng Palden Yeshi, his younger brother and administrator, appropriated his personal wealth without sharing it with Lama Chhodub Gyatso of the Shamar Karmapa Kangbachhen Monastery, an elder brother of the deceased Panchhen Lama. Lama

---

* Tibetan : Dejong (Bra ljongs), later Denzong.

Chhodub Gyatso, along with his entourage, went over to Nepal in order to score off his brother. The Nepalese court gave him asylum, and an estate.

Nepal invaded Tibet in the summer of 1788. The Gorkhas withdrew next year on certain terms. Nepal invoded Tibet again. Emperor Ch'ien Lung sent a large force under General Fu K'ang-an against Nepal. The Manchu court realized that the defeat of Tibet by the Gorkhas (Chin : Kuo-er-k'ao)might reduce it to the status of a vassal of Nepal. The Manchu force defeated the Nepalese force, chasing it almost to the gates of Kathmandu. The Gorkha court agreed not to raise any claim based on the coinage issue, return the property looted from the Tashilhunpo (Kra shis lhun po) Monastery and surrender the remains of the Shamar Lama, who had died in the meantime, and his wife and entourage. Above all, it also agreed to send an envoy to China every five years with presents for the Manchu emperor. Even the Nepal-Tibet war of 1855-56, which ended to the advantage of Nepal, did not change this pattern of relations between China and Nepal.

The Manchu court issued a set of imperial regulations authorizing its Amban at Lhasa to deal with the Dalai Lama directly and supervise his treasury without interfering with his personal funds. This strengthened the status of the Amban.The regulations also restricted the routing of all communications with foreign countries, especially Nepal, Sikkim and Bhutan, through him (Amban) and all correspondence addressed to the Dalai Lama by foreign countries to be made known to him, and replied by him. The Amban, however, was not to take part in the governance of Tibet.

Emperor Ch'ien Lung, as the patron of the Gelugpa Sect, also issued a decree concerning the procedure of the choice and appointment of the high Gelugpa lamas. Names of boys written on slips of paper were to be placed in a golden urn. The Dalai Lama, or the Panchhen Lama if the choice was that of the Dalai Lama, was to pick out a slip at random in the presence of the Amban and high Gelugpa dignitaries. The boy, whose name appeared on the slip, was to be appointed the high lama subject to the Manchu emperor granting him the patent of investiture. Later, the Manchu government also extended this procedure to the choice and appointment of the high Gelugpa lamas in Mongolia.

Tibet also got involved with Jammu in the early 1840s. General Zorawar Singh, who had taken Zangskar and Ladakh for Maharaja Ranjeet Singh (r. 1791-1839) of the Panjab in 1834, invaded West Tibet in May 1841, taking Rudok, Guge and Purang. He made Taglakhar his headquarters. He even posted his men close to the frontiers of Kumaun and Nepal. The Khenpo of the Shiwaling Monastery in Taglakhar escaped to Almora in British territory. The Tibetans, encircling the Dogra soldiers and shooting General Zorawar Singh, defeated the Dogras near Lake Mansarovar on 12 December 1841. Eventually, the Dogras rallied under Diwan Hari Chand and pursued the Tibetans. Tibet used for peace. The Dogras and the Tibetans concluded peace, which took the form of exchange of letters, on 17 September 1842. Those letters reaffirmed the old borders between Ladakh and Tibet, renewed the old trade connection between them and confirmed the authority of Jammu over Ladakh. The treaty established the *status quo* before the war, that is, Ladakh of Thondup Namgyal (r. 1820-34). Diwan Hari Chand took the representatives of Tibet (Kalon Surkhang and Pishi Shata) to Jammu, where the ratification took place.

Alexander Cunningham and Henry Strachey demarcated the Ladakh-Tibet border in 1847.

The treaty between China and Britain and France signed at Aigun on 27 June 1858 ratified by the convention signed at Peking on 24 October 1860, allowed Christian missionaries to travel and preach in the interior of China. The Roman Catholic Mission Etrangers (Lazarists) of Paris lost no time to penetrate into Kham. The treaties had not distinguished Tibet from China proper. This alarmed the Gelug dignitaries, and the government of Tibet forbade the entry of missionaries as well as travellers into Tibet. When the missionaries showed copies of the treaties of 1858 and 1860 to the Tibetan officials from Lhasa, they said they did not acknowledge the authority of the government of Emperor Sian Fang (r. 1851-62). The Manchu government had taken no part in the Jammu-Tibet war of 1841-42 and the Nepal-Tibet war of 1855-56; it then had been involved with the Westerners at the southern gates—the sea ports. It is, however, notable in this connection that the Manchu government sided with Nyarong in the Lhasa-Nyarong war of 1864-65. At any rate, the Tibetans were quite assertive then.

The first military clash Tibet had with a Western power occurred in Sikkim during the time of the young Dalai Lama Thubten Gyatso (1876-1933) on 21 March 1888. The British Indian troops drove the Tibetan troops out of Lingtu (gLing thar), chasing them up to Yatung across the Dzelep La in the Tomo (Gro mo) Valley, commonly known as the Chhumbi (Chhu mbi) Valley, inside Tibet. Had the government of Dalai Lama Thupten Gyatso taken proper notice of the British power then, it might have avoided the complications with the government of British India in the first years of this century.

The British and Manchu governments concluded a convention relating to Sikkim and Tibet and signed by Marquis Henry Charles Keith Lansdowne, the Viceroy and Governor-General of India from 1888 to 1894, and Sheng T'ai, the Manchu Amban in Tibet from 1890 to 1892, in Calcutta on 17 March 1890, recognizing the British protectorate over Sikkim and defining the Sikkim-Tibet border along the crest of the range, the upper reaches of the Teesta River. Sheng T'ai, who travelled from Lhasa to Calcutta and back, was the first Amban in Tibet to do so. He died in Lhasa in 1892.

The British and Manchu governments also signed at Darjeeling on 8 December 1893 a set of regulations relating to border trade, pasturage and communications. The Anglo-Chinese regulations of 1893 gave Yatung and its environments to the government of British India. The government of the Dalai Lama ignored the Anglo-Chinese convention and refused to comply with the regulations : it regarded Sikkim as its vassal.

The British government realized that the government of China had no authority in Tibet. It had also heard rumours of Russian influence in the counsels of Lhasa. Lord George Nathaniel Curzon of Kedleston, the Viceroy and Governor-General of India from 1899 to 1905, dispatched a mission (which later converted itself into a military expedition) to Tibet in the summer of 1903 to negotiate with the Dalai Lama. Sidkyong Tulku, the Maharaj Kumar (crown prince) of Sikkim, and Ugyen Wangchhuk, the *Ponlop* (dPon lop, Governor) of Tongsa, accompanied it. Dawa Penjor, the Ponlop of Paro and the cousin of Ugyen Wangchhuk, was then hostile to the government of British India. The Nepal-Tibet treaty of 1856 had bound Nepal to help Tibet in the event of an invasion.

However, Maharaja Chandra Shamsher, the Prime Minister of Nepal, offered yaks as transport animals to the British military expedition to Tibet.

When the expeditionary force advanced on Lhasa, Dalai Lama Thubten Gyatso, accompanied by Lama Agvan Dorjiev (1853-1938) of Buriyatia, Russia, escaped on 30 July 1904 to Manchu Mongolia where he hoped to gain Russian support. But Russian support was not available as the Russian government then had its own complications with Japan, fighting the war of 1904. Whatsoever, the Tibetan lamas and magicians could not prevent the penetration of the British Indian force into Tibet, and the parade of British bayonets in Lhasa.

The British and Tibetan officials signed a convention in the Potala at Lhasa on 7 August 1904 in the presence of Yer T'ai, the Manchu Amban in Tibet from 1902 to 1912, and the agents of Bhutan and Nepal. The Anglo-Tibetan Convention of 1904 affirmed the Anglo-Chinese Convention of 1890. It forbade Tibet to have relations with foreign powers. It limited the Manchu sovereignty in Tibet, but it continued to treat Manchu China as non-foreign. It allowed British trade agents to be established at Gyantse, and Gartok in West Tibet, in addition to Yatung where a British trade agent had been established under the Anglo-Chinese convention of 1890. It imposed an indemnity of Rs 75,00,000 on Tibet, later reduced to Rs 25,00,000 and the occupation of the Chhumbi Valley, south of the central ridge of the Himalaya (the Tibetans themselves suggested it) by the British government in lieu of the indemnity.

The Manchu government regarded the Anglo-Tibetan Convention as an imposition. But it signed a convention with the British government in Peking on 27 April 1906 to confirm the conventions of 1890 and 1904. By the Anglo-Chinese Convention of 1906, the British government recognized the suzerainty of Manchu China over Tibet. The Manchu government paid the indemnity on behalf of Tibet. The British government handed back the Chhumbi Valley to Tibet on 1 January 1908.

The Dalai Lama returned from Mongolia to Tibet in September 1906. While at the Kumbum Monastery in Amdo in North-East Tibet, he managed to visit Peking on 27 September 1908. He lodged in the Yellow Temple originally built, outside the north wall of the city, for Dalai Lama Lobzang Gyatso. Emperor Pu-i (r. 1908-12) and Dowager Empress Tz'u Hsi (Yehonala, 1835-1908) received him with respect. Their government gave him the title "loyal and submissive vice-regent" in place of his former title "Great, Good, Self-Existent Buddha". The Manchu government thus implied that Tibet was subordinate to Manchu China. The Dalai Lama, on his part, tried to imply that it was not so. It is noteworthy that he did not enjoy the prestige of Dalai Lama Lobzang Gyatso (1617-82), the first ever Dalai Lama to visit China.

At Peking, Dalai Lama Thubten Gyatso also met the diplomatic representatives of foreign countries. When he met the British representative, he said that he had been misinformed about British intentions in 1903-04 and that he now wished for friendship with Britain. This admission seems to have been more than polite diplomacy. He also addressed a letter to the British monarch, King Edward VII (r. 1901-10).

The Dalai Lama left Peking for Lhasa on 21 October 1908. The Manchu government sent to Tibet imperial troops from Ch'engtu (Szechwan) under Generals Chao Erh-feng and Lien-yu to enforce its authority. On the advance of the Manchu imperial troops on Lhasa on

12 February 1910 during the Losar Monlam Chhemmo festival, the Dalai Lama along with his entourage, fled to India. The Manchu government deposed him.

Manchu imperial troops even crossed the north-east frontier of India at several points and established the western limit of the Manchu empire at Menilkrai in the Sadiya frontier tract, the Lohit district of present-day Arunachal Pradesh. They did not farewell in the jagged principality of Po between Kongpo and Zayul, south-east Tibet. The Depa of Po escaped to Assam (India). The government of Assam kept him at Sadiya, the administrative headquarters of the Eastern and Central frontier tracts. There he married a Kamti, Buddhist woman, and had a daughter by her. He died on the east bank of the Dibang River, which rises on the east side of the Abroka Pass, in 1913 while returning to Kanam(Po) from Sadiya. The government of the Dalai Lama took Po in 1927 and merged it with Mar Kham in East Tibet.

The revolution in China on 10 October 1911 quickly spread to Tibet. Unpaid for months, the Chinese soldiers did enormous damage to life and property in Lhasa. The Tibetans besieged the Chinese garrison and routed the Chinese troops elsewhere in the country. Eventually, on 6 January 1913, except the merchants, Resident Chung-yin and the Chinese troops left Lhasa by way of Kalimpong in India. Yuan Shi-kai (1859-1916), President of the Republic of China founded by Dr Sun Yat-sen on 1 January 1912, voiced China's claim to Tibet. The government of President Yuan put Chung-yin to death in 1915 for leaving his post of duty against orders.

De Facto Autonomy

On return to Lhasa from India in the spring of 1912, Dalai Lama Thubten Gyatso issued a proclamation which the Tibetans regarded as the declaration of the independence of Tibet. The two escapes (1904-09) and (1910-12) of the Dalai Lama and varied experiences made him familiar with the complex of power politics in Central Asia. He sought to gain recognition of the independence of Tibet through the priest-patron relationship with another power. The British government could only offer mediation between Tibet and China. It held a Anglo-Chinese-Tibetan conference at Simla (now Shimla) in 1913-14 to resolve the question of the political status of Tibet. The tripartite conference split Tibet into two parts—Inner and Outer (as seen from China). Inner Tibet was to be directly under China and Outer Tibet was to be autonomous under the Dalai Lama, with a Chinese political agent stationed at Lhasa.

The Anglo-Chinese-Tibetan conference broke down because of the differences over definition of borders between China and Tibet. The tripartite delegates, however, initialled a draft agreement. The Dalai Lama was not happy with it. The government of the Republic of China (ROC) repudiated it. May it be noted that the government of China was reluctant to attend this conference in the first place. The British Government had convened it at a time when China was militarily prostrate. Anyway, the political status of Tibet vis-a-vis China remained unresolved. The British Government did not offer the sort of help to Tibet that the Russian government did to Mongolia. Tibet was not as important to Britain as Mongolia was to Russia.

The British and Tibetan delegations concluded an agreement respecting their common border from the Bhutan-India-Tibet trijunction to the India-Burma-China trijunction. It also extended 32 miles eastward up to the Isu Razi Pass on the Burma-China border. Burma was part of British India then. The Assam-Tibet border line came to be called the McMahon Line after the name of the British delegate and foreign secretary of the government of British India. Owing to the association of the Pemako(Padma bkoi)Valley, south of the central ridge of the Assam Himalaya, with the legendary Padmasambhava and for goodwill, the British Government conceded it to Tibet. The so-called McMahon Line has had an interesting run. China has never accepted it.

The aim of the government of the Dalai Lama of freedom from China made it vigorously assertive. But, due to the preoccupation of the British Government with the World War (1914-18), it was quiescent. Whatsoever, the Tibetan forces led by Kalon Lama Champa Tendor of Tibet defeated the Chinese forces in the hostilities along the China-Tibet border. As the result of unstable internal conditions, the authority of the government of the Republic of China had not strongly extended to its outlying provinces Sichuan and Yunnan. The British Government, committed to the settlement of the Sino-Tibetan issue, authorized its Consul Eric Teichman (in West China) to mediate between belligerent China and Tibet—the truce of Rongbatsa between General Liu Tsan-ting of China and Kalon Lama Champa Tendor of Tibet, August 1918, with the view to restore peace on the border pending the final settlement of the Sino-Tibeton bourdary dispute, The 1918 truce bourdary ran through Kham, with the Khamba people of the Tibetan race dwelling on both sides of it. The British authorities now omitted the words "Inner" and "Outer" in their discussions on Tibet with China.

On British advice, the government of Tibet started to modernize its army in the early 1920s. The question of one fourth contribution to be made by the Tashi-lhunpo Monastery in Shigatse resulted in much misunderstanding between the government of the Dalai Lama and the administration of the Tshilhunpo

Monastery. The officials, which Lhasa sent to Shigatse to demand the levy, perhaps misrepresented the matter. Panchhen Lama Chhokyi Nyima (1883-1937) as the head of the Tshilhunpo Monastery and its estates protested to Dalai Lama Thubten Gyatso. He felt that the levy made his position untenable. When his protest proved futile, he, along with a number of his officials, fled to China via the Changthang route on 15 November 1923. The government of the Republic of China received him warmly.

The Manchu government had always tried to reach the Panchhen Lama since 1727-28. It suspected the efforts of Panchhen Lama Lobzang Palden Yeshi (1737-80) to establish contacts with the government of the English East India Company (Calcutta), Maharaja Prithvinarayan Shah of Nepal and Raja Chait Singh of Varanasi (India) during the minority of Dalai Lama Jampel Gyatso (1758-1804) in the 1770s. His death in Peking was perhaps unnatural. Emperor Ch'ieng Lung had invited him in the context of the issue of the Torgot Mongols from the Volga region in Russia. The Manchu government also tried to set Panchhen Lama Chhokyi Nyima on the vacant throne in the Potala in the absence of Dalai Lama Thubten Gyatso in 1910. The Panchhen Lama did go over to Lhasa, but he did not take the seat of the Dalai Lama. When he sought shelter in China, whether he did so of his own volition or on the advice of his advisers is not important. What is important is the yet further complications it created for the Dalai Lama. The presence of the Panchhen Lama in China gave the government of China a powerful lever to restore its position in Tibet.

The Fifth Dalai Lama Lobzang Gyatso had conferred the title "Panchhen" (short for Pandita Chhenpo) on his and his predecessor's teacher Lama

Lobzang Chhokyi Gyaltsen and declared him to be the incarnation of Opamed/Amitabha. Historically, the relations between the Dalai Lama and the Panchhen Lama had always been cordial. The rift between Lhasa and Shigatse, however, began in 1910, when the Manchu government tried to set Panchhen Lama Chhokyi Nyima on the throne in the Potala. The attendants of the Panchhen Lama used the opportunity to develop relationships with the Manchu government in the hope of increasing their own influence. The Panchhen Lama, second only to the Dalai Lama in the Gelugpa hierarchy, himself had never been concerned with strictly secular matters apart from the administration of the districts and estates allocated for the support of his monasteries. His fiefs had always been part of the government of Tibet.

The flight of the Panchhen Lama seemed to have pained the Dalai Lama. Before passing on 17 December 1933, he strenuously strove for the return of the Panchhen Lama from China. He even opened negotiations with President Chiang Kai-shek to facilitate the return of the Panchhen Lama.

The government of the Republic of China, then in Nanking, sent General Huang Mu-sung to Lhasa to convey their condolence on the death of Dalai Lama Thubten Gyatso. It also authorized him to negotiate the status of Tibet as part of China. General Huang reached Lhass on 25 April 1934. Nothing, however, came out of his proposals and the counter-proposals of the Tibetan government. The obsequies over, Huang left Lhasa in October 1934, leaving behind Liu P'u-chen and Chang Wei-pei. He returned to China via Nepal and India. The government of the Republic of China, however, established Sikang Province in 1939. It consisted of Tibetan areas under its occupation since 1932. General Wu Chung-hsin (Chairman, Commission of Mongolian and Tibetan Affairs) travelled to Lhasa through India for the installation of the Fourteenth Dalai Lama Tenzin Gyatso on 22 February

1940. He established an office of the Commission of Mongolian and Tibetan Affairs in Lhasa, under Kung Ch'ing-tsung in April 1940.

The draft constitution of China of 1945 accorded special status to Tibet, along with Outer Mongolia.

On 8 July 1949, the Tibetan government asked Shen Tsun-lien, head of the office of the Commission of Mongolian and Tibetan Affairs in Lhasa, and other Chinese officials to leave Tibet. Perhaps it meant to demonstrate its neutrality in the civil war in China. In his book *Tibet And The Tibetans* (Stanford University Press, Stanford, 1952), Shen suggested home rule for Tibet.

Tenzing Gyatso, the sixteen-year old Fourteenth Dalai Lama, assumed his religious and secular power on the request of his government after the People's Liberation Army (PLA) of the People's Republic of China (PRC), founded by MaoZedong (1893-1976) and associates in Peking on 1 October 1949, entered Tibet on 7 October 1950. He had been the youngest Dalai Lama ever to assume his full power. He had no proper preparation for leading Tibet at its most critical time. The fall of Chhamdo, Kham, on 17 October 1950 compelled his government to seek terms with the Government of the People's Republic of China (PRC). On 18 December 1950, the Dalai Lama moved from Lhasa to Yatung, close to the Sikkim border, in order to be able to cross over to India, if necessary. When Mao Zedong proclaimed the People's Republic of China (PRC), he referred to a telegram from the 10-year old Panchhen Lama Kesang Tseten (1939-89) asking for the "liberation" of Tibet. On 5 September 1949, the boy Panchhen Lama had fallen into the hands of the Chinese communists.

Autonomous Region

The Chinese and Tibetan delegations concluded in Beijing (Peking) on 23 May 1951 a 17-point agreement on "Measures for the Peaceful Liberation of Tibet". This agreement placed the foreign relations, communications and defence of Tibet under the PRC Government. It provided autonomy to Tibet in its internal affairs. It separated religion and politics, but enjoined the PRC Government not to change the status of the Dalai Lama and other grand lamas of Tibet and not to interfere in the religious beliefs of the Tibetan people. The government of Tibet agreed to assist the PLA to consolidate the western defences of the People's Republic. The Panchhen Lama and his officials returned to Tibet after 28 years. The arrangement under the Sino-Tibetan agreement of 1951, the first written agreement between China and Tibet since the Chinese-Tibetan treaty of 821/822 AD, conformed with the arrangement between Mongol China and Tibet and between Manchu China and Tibet. The Republic of China and Tibet had reached no understanding.

Recapitulating Theocracy

The family of the Seventh Dalai Lama was the first to be ennobled. The Eighth Dalai Lama was the first Dalai Lama to address a communication to the British government in India. The families of the Eighth and Twelfth Dalai Lamas united in matrimony. The Ninth-Twelfth Dalai Lamas played no notable part in the life of Tibet. Several of them died before they came of age to assume full power. The visit of Thomas Manning to Tibet in 1811 was the highlight of the time of the Ninth Dalai Lama, Lungtok Gyatso. Manning was the first Englishman to reach Lhasa and the first Westerner to have an audience with a Dalai Lama except for Ippolito Desideri, the Italian Jesuit, who had an audience with the puppet Dalai Lama of Lobzang Khan. The Thirteenth Dalai Lama came to power at a critical moment in the history of Central Asia. He became involved in the politics of Anglo-Russian contest for supremacy in Central Asia then. The present Fourteenth Dalai Lama was the youngest Dalai Lama to assume power. All the Dalai Lamas from the Seventh to the Fourteenth have been from ordinary peasant families. All this, especially how these peasant ordinary families transformed into royal families, is fescinating sociologically.

Autonomous Region of PRC

The advance of the PLA into Tibet to liberate it from feudal stranglehold created a rift between the governments of the Republic of India and People's Republic of China over the sovereign/suzerain position of China in Tibet. Delhi suggested the solution of the problem by peaceful means. Beijing resented it, regarding it as India's interference in China's internal affairs. Indian diplomacy failed to convey properly the concern of the Government of India to the PRC Government in the matter. On 8 September 1952, the Government of India changed its Mission in Lhasa to Consulate General under the jurisdiction of its Embassy in Beijing, and its Trade Agencies in Tibet under its supervision. On 29 April 1954, it concluded with the Government of the People's Republic of China in Beijing an agreement on trade and communications between India and the Tibet Region of China by which it gave up its rights in Tibet which it had inherited as the successor of the British government in India on 15 August 1947. It also withdrew its military escorts from its Trade Agencies in Yatung and Gyantse and handed over its rest-houses and post and telegraph facilities to the authorities of the People's Government in Tibet. The most important part of the agreement was the acceptance of Tibet, in the preamble, by the Govern-ment of India as an integral part of China.

Dalai Lama Tenzing Gyatso, along with Panchhen Lama Kesang Tseten, came to India on 23 November 1956 to take part in the celebrations of the 2500th

Buddha anniversary. He did not want to return to Tibet. The situation in Tibet was not normal then. He asked Prime Minister Jawaharlal Nehru for asylum in India. The request of the Dalai Lama was embarrassing to the Government of India for several reasons, not the least of which was that it had given assurances to the PRC Government that the visit of the Dalai Lama could neither be used nor allowed to be used for political intrigue.

Prime Minister Jawaharlal Nehru spoke to Prime Minister Chou Enlai, who happened to be in India then. Chou said to Nehru that the PRC Government would respect Tibetan autonomy in accordance with the Sino-Tibetan agreement of 1951. So on Nehru's suggestion that the situation in Tibet might improve, the Dalai Lama hesitatingly returned to Tibet. He also invited Nehru himself to see the situation there. In view of the situation in Tibet then, the PRC Government asked Nehru to cancel his visit. Perhaps it had no alternative.

An uprising against the Chinese rule (beginning in Amdo and Kham, North-East Tibet, especially after the reform of 1956) erupted in Lhasa on 10 March 1959. The Dalai Lama escaped from there in the night on 17 March. On entering India on 31 March, he requested for asylum for himself and for his entourage. The Dalai Lama and his entourage repudiated the Sino-Tibetan agreement of 1951 when they fled Tibet. W.D. Shakabpa even wrote a book—*Tibet : a political history* (Yale University Press, New Haven, Conn., 1967) expressing the views of the old guard. Apart from the aspirations of the Tibetans for freedom from China, the Dalai Lama seems, willy-nilly, to have then become a tool in the Western design to disintegrate the People's Republic of China. Perhaps the US design traced to the visit of Lowell Thomas and his son to Tibet in mid-August 1949.

The Government of India provided a comfortable house to the Dalai Lama, first at Mussoorie and then at Dharamshala. After decades of arrival in India, the Dalai Lama sent five fact-finding delegations to Beijing and Tibet between 1979 and 1985. He made a five-point proposal before the US Congress in Washington DC in 1987 and the European Parliament in Strasbourg (France) on 15 June 1988 for autonomy for Tibet within the framework of the People's Republic of China, and repeated it frequently. On 20 March 1989, Beijing said : "Any issue is open for discussion except the question of Tibetan independence", and repeated it frequently. Persident Jiang Zemin, uring his a-day state visit to the Uinted States of America from 26 October to 3 November 1997, publicly emphasized in different places and under different auspices, the inseparability and inalienability of Tobet from China. He also emphasised the issue of human rights in Tibet as an internal affair of China. That is that. Whatsoever, for the Dalai Lama asylum in India has not been dreary.

The PRC Government organized Tibet as an autonomous region on 30 September 1965, the central and western parts of Tibet constituting the autonomous region. Besides its programme of economic and social reforms, the PRC Government constructed highways to link Tibet with China proper. Beijing's effort to integrate Tibet into the mainstream of the People's Republic of course has not been free from resistance.

The takeover of Tibet by the PRC Government has been, in a way, a blessing in disguise. The Buddhist culture of Tibet has become known, in an unprecedented way, throughout the world. Since then, thousands of Tibetans have left the country. And whatever the politics, they may never return to their native land.

3

XINJIANG : DUNES AND OASES

Xinjiang is an ancient land of non-indigenous people. It is the Far West of China. It has had much variable history. It has had different names in history. Its present name Xinjiang Uigur Region is from 1955. It will be no distortion of history to name it *Xiyu*, the Western Territory, or such name.

The Hsiung-nu/Huna, Hsian-pei and other northern tribes constantly inroaded into Han China. Emperor Wu Ti (reign 141-86 B.C.) of the first, Western Han dynasty (206 B.C.-A.D. 4) sent his minister Prince Ch'ang Ch'ien twice during 141-115 B.C. to the Yueh-chih/Kushana tribe, who had been defeated by Motun (r. 209 B.C.-174 B.C.), the son of Tumen* of the Hsiung-nu tribe, in 176 B.C. and who had been driven westwards from their homeland in Gansu (Kansu) during the time of Shan-yu Chichu (r. 174-160 B.C.). He had aimed to form an alliance with the Yueh-chih against the Hsiung-nu. Ch'ang reached the Yueh-chih in *circa* 128 B.C. He did not succeed in his aim. The Hsiung-nu captured him but gave him a wife. He returned to China in 128 B.C.

Whatsoever, Ch'ang Ch'ien was the first Chinese to visit Hsi Yu, the Western Region. Emperor Wu signed the *ho-ch'in* treaty with Shan-yu Chun-ch'en (r. 160-126 B.C.), the grandson of Motun, in 135 B.C. He sent them lavish gifts and allowed them to trade in the border markets. The region of present-day Xinjiang, which first opened up to China during the first Han dynasty has ever since remained in its manifest or vague possession.

---

* The first *Shan-yu,* the Great Chief of the Hsiung-nu tribe.

The geographical connection between China and Central Asia, forged by Ch'ang Ch'ien, led to the establishment of the caravan route, later called the "Silk Road", between East and West in BC 115. Ferdinand Freiherr von Richthofen, the German geographer-explorer, was the first to use the evocative term for this route. The Silk Road brought ancient China and imperial Rome in a sort of relationship. It carried silk, spices, jade and other goods, but mainly silk, from China to the countries of the Mediterranean Sea and glassware, iron, precious stones and other goods from there to China. Roman coins had not gained currency in Central Asia then. Rome sent bullion instead. The Silk Road was also the road of pilgrimage and religious teaching. It thus carried not only silk and bullion but also civilization. Of course, there was nothing silky about the Silk Road. On the other hand, it was most dangerous, and hazardous.

The caravan route between China and the Mediterranean world had two branches, the northern and the southern, which started at the oasis town of Dunhuang (Tunhuang) in the heart of the Gobi Desert in Gansu though the Gansu/Western Corridor beyond the Yellow River and came together at Kashgarh* (Chin : Su-le). From Kashgarh it continued westwards across the Fargana (later pronounced Fergana; Chin: Ta Yuan) and the Pamir valleys to Balkh and Bukhara and, via Persia and Mesopotamia, to the Mediterranean. The Balkh branch connected it with India. The two branches joined at Marv (pronounced Merv). The present east-west highway across Xinjiang follows the ancient Silk Road from Hami (Ha-mi, Uigur : Komul) in the east to Turfan (Turpan, Chin : Hsi-chen, Tulufan) at the edge of the Gobi Desert in the west.

* Kashgar of the maps, dropping final "h".

East Central Asia was the key to the foreign policy of China of the Han dynasty, dictated by the need to contain nomad presssure. The conquest of Fargana by General Li Kuang-li in 101 B.C. led to the elimination of the Hsiung-nu from the Western Region, and the establishment of China's sway there. General Cheng Chi set up the office of *Hsi-yu Tu-hu*, the Protector-General of the Western Region, in 60 B.C.. The Han court appointed him Hsi-yu Tu-hu. Emperor Mingti (r. A.D. 57-75) of the second, Eastern Han dynasty (A.D. 25-220) took measures to guard the Silk Road and other caravan routes through Eastern Central Asia. General Tu Ku reduced the kings and princes of the 36 oasis kingdoms of the Tarim region between the Kuenlun and Tianshan ranges. He sent Pan Ch'ao (32-92 A.D.) to re-establish the office of the Protector-General at Kucha (Chin : Ch'iu-tzu) in 73-74. After the fall of the Mongol Yuan dynasty (1271-1368) of China, the Chinese position in Central Asia had been tenuous.

Oasis Kingdoms

The kingdoms of the Western Region began to come into existence before the end of the 2nd century B.C. From towards the end of the reign of Emperor Kuang-wu (A.D. 25-57) to about 73, several of them rose to power. The first kingdom, which became a dominant force, in the Western Region, was Sha-ch'a/Yarkand. The king of Sha-ch'a (named Hsien in Chinese, r. 33-61), even tried to take the entire Western Region. Other kingdoms also contended for supremacy there. Yu-tien/Khotan subdued Sha-ch'a. Emperor Kuang-wu's inability, owing to internal conditions in China then, to intervene enabled the Hsiung-nus to establish their power there. Pan Yung, the son of General Pan Ch'ao, made efforts to recover the Western Region from them.

General Tu Ku defeated the Hsiung-nus in 74. He took Yu-tien, Sha-ch'a and Shu-le between 73 and 100. China had captured Andijan, the capital of Fargana, and imposed an indemnity of 1,000 stallions in 104-102 B.C. It had set up, within its military establishment, an office of horse purchase that dealt directly with the pastoral suppliers of horses. Its writ, though nominal, then ran up to the Kushana domain.

The Arabs under Ziyad b. Salih, the general of Abu Muslim (official name Abdal-Rahman b. Muslim) of the Abbasid Khilafat of Baghdad, routed the army of General Kao Hsien-chin (of Korean origin) in the battle of Taraz (later Auli Ata, now Jambul named after the Kazak poet Jambul) to the west of Bishkek, the capital of present-day Kirgizstan, on the Talas River in July 751. China withdrew from Fargana to its strongholds in the Western Region. Its interest in the lands to its north and west was to protect itself from incursions of the five non-Han nomadic tribes* there.

The rule of Tibet in Liyul, the collective Tibetan name for the Khotan-Kashgarh region, in the seventh-ninth centuries, extended over the people of Indo-Iranian origin. The kings of the oasis-kingdoms bore Sanskrit names. The location of the city Kingdom of Khotan (Ku-sa-ta-na) on the Silk Road gave it prosperity. Archaeological expeditions sponsored by the government of British India and the Count Kojui Otani of Japan in the beginning of the present century, dug up the great past of this sand-burried ancient kingdom. Their literary finds shed much light on ancient China, India and Iran. According to a legend of the Buddhism of Central Asia, Prince Kunal, a son of Emperor Ashoka (r. 369-332 B.C.) of India, founded

---

*Referred to, in the history of ancient China, as Siung-nu, Sian-pie, Jie, Ti and Ch'iang.

Khotan. Buddhism spread there in the first century A.D., in 84 B.C. according to the *Li yul long btsan pa/ Li yul chhos gyi lo rgyus*, the annals of Liyul. Emperor Ming Ti (r. A.D. 58-76) sent a mission to Khotan in 65 A.D. for acquiring Buddhist monks and texts. The Buddhist monks such as Kumarajeeva (d. 413) of Kucha influenced the development of Buddhism even in China.

Kumarajeeva had studied in Kashmira (Kashmir). His mother Jeeva, a Tokharika*, had taken him there. His father was from Kashmira. He reached Chang'an (now Xian), the capital of the then China in the Wei River Valley, in 401 and engaged himself in the work of translation of Sanskrit Buddhist texts into Chinese, including *Ma-ming pu-sa-chuan*, the life of Ashvaghosa. According to the tradition of the Buddhism of China, he so impressed Emperor Yao Chang (r. 386-417)** of the Topa Wei dynasty (386-556) that he (Emperor Yao Chang) assigned ten girls to live with him (Kumarajeeva) so that his qualities of mind should be transmitted to offspring. And children were born. Kumarajeeva said to his associates : "You need only take the lotus that grows out of the mud and leave the mud".

Khotan, a major stage place on the Silk Road up to 1000 A.D., was a tributary of China until its conquest by the Tibetans in 670. The people of many races met there. The Chinese and the Indians first met there. The people speaking Indo-Iranian languages lived in the city-kingdoms. When, after the collapse of their empire (744-840) in the Orkhon region, the Uigurs (Chin Hui-hu of the Chinese sources), had moved to Gansu and risen to power in the Taklamakan-

---

* A woman of Kucha. Kucha came under China in 640 AD. It became an Uigur kingdom after the fall of the T'ang dynasty of China.

** The Ch'in dynasty unified China in 221 B.C. and constructed the Great Wall to keep out the Siung-nus.

Tarim region, they absorbed the Indo-Iranian speaking peoples. Some of the Indo-Iranian peoples withdrew into the fastnesses of the Pamir mountains. The Uigurs adopted Buddhism after they had moved to Turpan in the west.

Karakhan Dynasty

The Karluk Turks established the Karakhan dynasty (*c.* 940-1125) at Balasagun in the Chu River Valley. Satuk Bugra Khan (*d.* 955) was the first prince of the Karakhan dynasty to convert to Islam in 945. Kadir Khan (r. 1015-32) of the right or eastern part of the Karakhan domain*, the supreme Karakhan ruler, spread it eastwards from Kashgarh. The Khotanis resisted for long the advance of Islam. Arslan Khan (r. 1032-55), who led the Muslim forces, died in the last battle. But his forces won. The place of his death, later called *Ordam Padshah*, the Place of King, became a place of pilgrimage. Most of the Buddhist monks escaped to Tibet and China. The Karakhans are the "Ilikhs" of the Arab travellers.

Before the advent of Islam, the languages of the Tarim basin were not Turki. The Uigur dialect was the first Turki dialect to be reduced to alphabet writing in the time of Muhammad Bugra Khan II (r. 1057-1102). It eventually acquired the status of Eastern Turki. The Uigur script developed from the Sugdi script. The Kitan and Mongol scripts developed from it. Mahmud al-Kashgarhi, a Karakhan scion, wrote his dictionary *Diwan Lughat at-Turk* in the Arabic language and script in Baghdad in 1072**. Kashgarhi's *Lughat* is, except for place names, an encyclopaedia, a storehouse of information on the ethnography and history of the Turks of Central Asia up to his time.

---

* The Karakhan dynasty followed the early Turk imperial practice of the bipartite system of rule. The Karakhan court moved its political centre to Kashgarh in the 11th century.

** Kashgarhi had escaped the intra-dynasty fighting in which his father Husain had been killed.

The period of the Karakhan dynasty is noteworthy for the creation of Turki literature, for instance the *Kudatku Bilik* (Mirror for Princes) of Hajip Yusuf Khan of the court of Muhammad Bugra Khan. Written in verse in Turki in Kashgarh in 1070, it related to the duties of a ruler to his people. Hajip Yusuf was born in Balasagun.

Qarakitai Dynasty

The Qarakitais* of the Yeh-lu clan of the Kitan tribe of East Asia overthrew Mahmud Khan of the Karakhan dynasty. Yelu (born 1086; r. 1125-36), the head of the Qarakitai dynasty (1125-1211), took the title *Gur Khan*, the Universal Lord. The Qarakitais dominated even Samarkand and Bukhara up to 1211, when Allaheddin Muhammad, the Khwarazm (pronounced Khorezm) Shah killed Osman, the vassal of the Qarakitai Gurkhan, and overlorded it. The Qarakitais were first tributary to Sultan Sanjar (r. 1092-1157) of the Saljuk Turk dynasty (1038-1157) of Khurasan** and Iran, but defeated him in 1141. They had not yet adopted Islam.

The armies of Chingiz/Chinggiz Khan (*b.* 1167, r. 1206-27) poured into China and Persia, invaded Russia, Poland and Moravia and reached Hungary and Austria***. The Mongols under General Jebe took the Taklamakan-Tarim region in 1218 without much resistance and destruction. Guchuk, the son of Taiyeng

---

* Tungus Hsi Liao; Karakitai of the Persian authors. Emperor U-tu-bu of the Ch'in dynasty of North China overthrew the Liao dynasty (916-1125).

** Khurasan stretched, and stretches, from the Amu Darya-Hindu Kush range in the east to Jajram, south-east of the Caspian Sea.

*** In the 13th century, China or rather North China became known in Europe as Cathay or Catai, a name derived from the ethnic term Kitan. It still survives as the general name for China in most Slavonic languages, e.g., in Russian *Kitai*. The Kitans conquered China in 907 and held it up to 1124. The Juchen (Jurchen) overthrew them in 1129.

Khan of the Naiman Turk tribe, who had fled to Gurkhan Jilegu (r. 1199-11) of the Qarakitai dynasty in 1208 after the break-up of the Naiman power by Chingiz Khan in 1204, was then at Kashgarh. Jilegu had given him (Guchuk) his daughter in marriage. Guchuk even adopted the Qarakitai dress and customs, and adopted Buddhism. After becoming powerful, he overthrew Gurkhan Jilegu in 1211. Jebe pursued Guchuk Khan and killed him.

Mogolistan

Chingiz Khan divided his vast empire, stretching from the Pacific Ocean in the east to Central Europe in the west and from Siberia in the north to Burma (Myanmar now) in the south, among his sons and grandsons about 1224. He gave the Middle Mongol Empire of the Taklamakan-Tarim and Mawa 'ra an-nahr to Chagatai, his second son, as his appange with Almalik in the Tianshan range as his headquarters. Within a century of Chagatai's death, the Middle Mongol Empire broke up into eastern and western parts. Togon Temur (b.1335; r.1347-68), who ascended the throne of the eastern part and converted himself to Islam with the name of Tuglak Temur, named it Mogolistan.

The policy of the Mings of the Ming dynasty (1368-1644), who ousted the Mongols from China, was not assertive in the Taklamakan-Tarim region. Khizr Khoja (r. 1389-99), the Sultan of Mogolistan, and Kamareddin Duglat*, the general of Khizr Khoja and Amir of Kashgarh, got involved with Emir (Amir) Timur of Samarkand during his campaign in Fargana. Emir Timur himself never went east beyond Andijan, Fargana : he sent his expeditions to Mogolistan.

---

* The Duglat family had been the hereditary ruler of Kashgarh under the Mogol khans.

Sultan Sa'id Khan (d. 1457) brought peace to Mogolistan. Of his two sons Saniz and Hayder, Saniz (r. 1457-64) made Yarkand his capital and assigned Kashgarh to Hayder. He died of a fall from his horse. When Abu Bakr Duglat became Amir of Kashgarh, he tried to extend his sovereignty over all Mogolistan. He annexed Osh in Fargana, and invaded even Andijan. Mir Vali, the general of Abu Bakr, reputedly conquered even Badakshan and Gilgit. Sultan Ahmad (r. 1499-1503) set out against Abu Bakr, and took Kashgarh. He died at Aksu. History knows him by his alias Alaja, the Slayer, because he rid Mogolistan of internecine strife.

The 17 sons of Alaja quarrelled over the sovereignty of Mongolistan. Except Abu Sa'id Khan, Mansur Khan (r. 1503-12) subdued them. He and Abu Sa'id agreed to share the sovereignty of Mogolistan on the condition that the *khutba*, the sermon in the Juma' *namaz*, Friday prayer, be delivered and coins be struck in the name of Mansur Khan.

Sultan Abu Sa'id Khan (r. 1512-33) aimed to seek Abu Bakr. He was with Zahiruddin Babur (1483-1530) at Kabul in 1504. With Babur, he returned to Kunduz. Abu Bakr had invaded Andijan with a large force. Abu Sa'id Khan had a small force. By sheer determination, he defeated Abu Bakr near Andijan.

Sultan Abu Sa'id deputed his son Abder Rashid (born at Andijan in 1506), and Muhammad Hayder to conduct *Jihad* , holy war, against Tibet. General Muhammad Hayder had entered his service as a soldier in 1526. Abder Rashid returned to Yarkand in 1527. General Hayder reached the Nubra Valley, north-west of Leh, in Ladakh in 1532. Gyalpo Tashigon (*d.* 1532) ruled Ladakh then. Sultan Sa'id, who also reached Nubra, then ordered Hayder to invade

Baltistan and Kashmir. Sultan* Ibrahim Shah (r. 1516-37) of the Chak Turk Afghan dynasty of Kashmir agreed to be a feudatory of Sultan Sa'id. He also agreed to mention the name of Sultan Sa'id in the *khutba* in the Friday prayer and strike coins in his name.

A rift between Muhammad Hayder and Daim Ali compelled Muhammad Hayder to return to Baltistan. Sultan Sa'id, who was ill, confided to Hayder his illness : he suffered from breathlessness. He himself hastened towards Yarkand, dying near the Karakoram Pass in 1533. The Karakoram camping ground came to be named after his title "Daulat Be", the Lord of State.Meanwhile, Abder Rashid (r. 1533-65/6), took Kashgarh by killing his uncle Muhammad and the family and expelling Hayder from the country and ordering the Mogol soldiers under him to return home. Before Hayder deputed his emissaries to Sultan Abder to change his decision, most of his soldiers deserted him.

After many wanderings, Hayder found shelter with Mirza/Prince Kamran, the second son of Zahiruddin Babar, at Lahore. After defeating Sultan Ibrahim Lodi (r. 1517-26) in the battle of Panipat on 20 April 1526, Babar had founded the Mughal (Mogol) dynasty, and empire. Humayun (r. 1531-40, 1555-56) had appointed Mirza Kamran as the viceroy of Lahore, Kabul and Kandahar. Kamran, who had sent an expedition against Kashmir in 1531, deputed Hayder to annex it. Hayder, who already had the experience of an expedition against Kashmir, entered Kashmir without any resistance. After consolidating his position, he deposed Sultan Ibrahim Shah, replacing him by Nazuk Shah (r. 1529-30) as his own nominee. Hayder

---

* The Sultanate period of Kashmir, 1320-1586.

(*d.* 1551) recounted in his *Tarikh-i Rashidi* the history of Central Asia during 1347-1542. Although a Turk of the Dugla't clan of Kashgarh, he wrote it in Persian in Srinagar in 1546.

Sultan Abder Rashid obtained the support of the Uzbek Khans through matrimonial relations with their nobles. He had two sons : Abdul Karim (r. 1565-93) and Muhammad Khan. However, after his death, the Chagatai Khanate of Mogolistan eventually disintegrated and disappeared as a result of the internecine quarrels in the Chagatai royal family.

Khoja Advent

A Khoja (Khwaja)* family from Mawarannahar rose in Mogolistan during the reign of Sultan Abder Rashid. A Sufi saint, Khoja Ahmad Kasani 1461-1543, known as Makhtum-i A'zam, the Great Teacher, of the Emirate of Bukhara and a son of Shaykh Ubaydullah Ahrar (1404-90), came to Kashgarh, allegedly on the invitation of Sultan Abder Rashid. He claimed descent from Prophet Muhammad. He died in Kashgarh. Among his sons, who enjoyed respect by virtue of their descent, Muhammad Amin, known as Imam-i Kalan, the Great Imam, established himself at Aktag, north of Kashgarh in the Tianshan range, and styled himself as Aktaglik, the White Mountaineer. Ishak, the younger brother of Muhammad Amin, established himself as Kartaglik, the Black Mountaineer. Not content with religious authority, both clans aspired for political power in Kashgarhia. By the end of the seventeenth century, they displaced the descendants of Chagatai Khan as rulers in Kashgarhia and themselves assumed rule there. They based their power on theocratic foundation.

---

* The title of the pioneers of the Nakshbandiyya Sufi order.

Hidayatullah alias Hazrat Afak/Apak*, the leader of the Aktaglik clan, sought the support of Galdan Khan (r. 1664-97) of the Khanate of the Oirat Mongols in the Ili River Valley, Galdan Khan, taking advantage of the situation, captured Khan Isma'il, the Mogol Khan of Kashgarh, and his family and exiled them to Kulja, his capital on the Ili River, in 1678. He appointed Hazrat Apak his representative at Kashgarh. He occupied Hami (Komul) in 1679. Before leaving Kashgarh, he (Galdan Khan) appointed an Oirat governor at Yarkand and posted his garrisons in the cities and towns of the oases of the Taklamakan—Tarim region. This abolished the Chagatai Mogolistan.

The partisans of Hazrat Apak did not feel satisfied with this arrangement. Instead of becoming independent, Kashgarhia had become subordinate to another country. So Apak thought of another stratagem in order to free himself of the stigma of betrayal. He invited Muhammad Amin, the brother of Isma'il of Uch Turpan to deliver the country from the Oirat Mongol yoke. This act of Apak's caused misfortunes greater than his betrayal. Kashgarhia became the arena of struggle between the Aktaglik and Karataglik factions. Apak died in mysterious circumstances in 1693/4. People still revere his name. His mausoleum—the Mosque of Hazrat Apak— and the grave site of the family—Khoja Apak—at Kashgarh became a source of wealth to the Aktaglik Khoja family from pilgrim offerings.

The rivalry between the Khoja factions continued even after the death of Apak. Hazrat Apak's wife, Khanum Padshah, slew, with the help of his disciples, Apak's eldest son, who had to become the leader of the Aktagliks. She had wanted her son Mehdi to

---

* *Afak/Apak* is Turki for "snow", "pure white", that is, holy.

become the head of the Aktagliks. In the struggle, she herself became the victim of a follower. The Karatagliks pressed the claim of Daniyal, their leader. They arrested Ahmad, the leader of the Aktagliks, and his family. After the death of Daniyal, Galdan Khan divided Kashgarhia among the sons of Daniyal. Yusuf wanted to secure independence for the country. He sent emissaries to Kokand and Bukhara to seek help to oust the infidel Oirat Mongols in the name of Islam.

Due to the struggle for the position of Khan of the Khanate of Zungaria, Amursana (1717/18-57; Chin: A-mu-l-sa-na), a distant relative of the royal family of the Zungar Khanate, connived with the rulers of Manchu China to secure the position for himself. A Manchu force, which marched into the Ili Valley under his guidance, took it. Amursana also devised a scheme for the conquest of Kashgarhia. Taking advantage of the conflict between the Khoja factions, he instigated Burha'neddin and Khoja Khan, the sons of Hazrat Apak, to regain their position. A large force consisting of the Manchus and Oirat Mongols and the followers of Burhaneddin under General Fute marched against Kashgarh in 1759. Yusuf Khoja of the Karataglik faction, organized a force to oppose it. He died at Yarkand. The Karatagliks installed his son with the title "Padshah".

The Black and White Khoja factions proposed to unite in the name of Islam, and, instead of fighting each other, invade Kulja. By way of inducement the Karatagliks offered Kashgarh, Aksu and Turpan to Burhaneddin. Instead of agreeing to this proposal, Burhaneddin negotiated with Amursana and attacked the Karataglik forces.

Manchu Primacy

The perfidy of Burhaneddin and others were opportune for the Manchus to advance into the Taklamakan-

Tarim region. They executed the Khoja (Chin : Ho-cho) leaders and granted favours to the Muslim nobles loyal to them. They assigned Aksu to Saifuti Beg, Kucha to Islam Beg, Kashgarh to Gati Beg, Yangi Hissar to Ak Beg, Yarkand to Huti Beg and Khotan to Niyaz Beg. They accepted the conditions of loyal Muslims : no interference in their religious matters.

The Manchus, however, could not pacify the Oirat Mongols until the campaign of Emperor Ch'ien Lung (r. 1736-96; *d.* 1799), the fourth emperor of Manchu China, against Amursana. Amursana, who had formerly been the Manchu *amban* (governor) of Uliasutai in West Mongolia, had rebelled against them. He had aspired to become the Khan of the Zungar Khanate. The Manchus had denied him that position. In order to fulfil his ambition, he sought an alliance with the Khalkha insurgents under the Zasagtu Khan Chingunjav against the Manchus. He also sought help from Russia. The stipulations of the Sino-Russian treaty, signed at Kiakhta (Chin : Ch'ia-k'o-ta) on the Mongolian-Russian border on 14 June 1727, perhaps restrained the Russian government to accept his request. But it assured him of welcome should he seek asylum in Russia. Thereupon, along with his family and followers, he escaped to Siberia, dying of small-pox in the environs of Tobol'sk, the capital of Siberia on the Tobol River, on 21 September 1757.

After the conquest of the Zungar Khanate, the Manchu army wiped out most of the Oirat Mongols. Thus the fate of Amursana fundamentally changed the situation in East Asia. It completed the process of Manchu conquest of the Mongols excepting the Buriyat Mongols of Siberia. After the conquest of Kashgarhia, Emperor Ch'ien Lung bestowed Chinese names upon its principal cities.

Amursana's followers returned to their homeland in the Ili Valley along with the Torgot Mongols returning from the Ural-Volga region, led by Ubasa (Ubasi) Khan (r. 1761-71, d. 1774), in 1771-72. The Torgots had wandered from the Ili Valley to the Lower Volga region in 1617, 1675 and 1703. Tsar Peter the Great (r. 1689-1725) had allowed them to occupy the steppes between the Emba and Volga rivers. The Torgots started their long trek from Russia on 1 January 1771. Emperor Ch'ien Lung rehabilitated them in the valley of the Kash River, the major right affluent of the Ili River. The Torgots, who remained in the Ural-Volga region, came to be known as the Kalmuks.

Formation of Sinkiang

The Manchu government of China annexed all the lands from the Gobi Desert in the east to the Pamir mountains in the west and from the Altai range in the north to the K'uenlun range in the south and named them Sinkiang (Hsinkiang), "New Territory", north and south of the Tianshan range. Kashgarhia (Chin : Hu-pu), the southern half of Sinkiang, was much bigger than Zungaria, its northern half, Strategically, Zungaria was more important than Kasgarhia. Zungaria was the westward extension of Mongolia in the context of Kobdo and Uliasutai in the Altai mountains. For the administration of Sinkiang, the Manchu government established the office of *Chiang-chin*. "Military governor", at Kulja in the Ili Valley in 1762. The *Tu-tung*. "Command generals" at Urumtsi* and Yarkand assisted the Chiang-chin. The office of Chiang-chin was also the military district for the western frontier of the Manchu empire.

---

* A Dzungar place-name. Situated in a fertile valley, it lies on a northern spur of the Eastern Tianshan.

The Manchu government also moved Manchu (Shibo and Solon) and Mongol troops together with their families from China and Mongolia to garrison Kulja and man the northwest frontier of the empire. They arrived as military settlers in the Ili Valley in 1764.

The Manchu Emperor Abahai (*b.* 1582; r. 1623-43), the eighth son of Nurhachi (*b.* 1559; r. 1616-26), subdued the Eastern Chahar Mongols in 1631, defeating Ligdan Khan (r. 1604-34), their chieftain and the last khan of all Mongols. He assumed the dignity of Emperor at Mukden and changed the dynastic title "Hou Chin", to "Ch'ing" on 14 May 1636, He had given the title "Hou Chin" to his dynasty in 1616. The Manchu court set up a bureau to superintend Korean and Mongol affairs in 1637. This bureau then became *Li Fan Yuan*, the Bureau of Tibet and Mongolia (and Sinkiang since 1761)—the Court of Colonial Affairs of the Western literature on China. Its establishment was an important measure.

After the absorption of Kashgarhia and Zungaria in the Manchu empire, a considerable mass of the Dungan (Tungan)—Chinese in dress, manners and customs—and Tranchi (Uigurs from the Ili country) people fled to Fargana and Jetusu. This emigration continued until the 1880s, when the Uigurs fled Kulja after the Russian withdrawal from the Ili country. Those Uigurs had sided with the Russians during their occupation of the Ili country in 1871-79.

When the Manchus suppressed the Khojas and took Khotan in 1760, Sarimsak, a son of Burhaneddin, escaped to Kokand. His followers and emigrants from Kashgarh joined him. Sarimsak put to them his scheme to deliver their homeland from the Manchu yoke. As the descendant of Hazrat Apak, he issued a *fatwa* for *Jihad* holy war against the infidel Manchus. Jahangir

(1789-1828), the son of Sarimsak, attempted to restore Khoja rule over Kashgarhia in the 1820s. In 1822, he fled from Kashgarh to the Kirgiz, where the Khojas had their following. He assumed the role of *imam* to deliver them from the Manchu Yoke. The Manchu amban of Kashgarh sent a force against Jahangir in 1825. The force of Jahangir massacred it. The people hailed his victory as the victory of Islam. Jahangir established himself in the palace of the khans of Kashgarh. He adopted the name of Sayyid, descendant of Prophet Muhammad.

Muhammad Amin (r. 1822-42), the Khan of the Khanate of Kokand, regarded Sayyid Jahangir as his preceptor. He placed at Jahangir's disposal the services of his General Isa Dadka together with a contingent of horsemen. He himself came to Kashgarh to offer his allegiance. But Jahangir seems to have shown him slight courtesy.

A Manchu force from Aksu marched towards Kashgarh in 1827. Jahangir fled Kashgarh. His friend Muhammad, perhaps out of fear of the Manchu attack, handed him over to General Yung Feng of the Manchu force on 14 February. They sent him to Peking in an iron cage like a beast—the usual form of punishment in China for centuries. The Manchus re-established their authority in Kashgarh in the spring of 1828.

The Khoja revolt against the Manchus had originated in the Khanate of Kokand. The Manchus had imposed a trade blockade against the Khanate of Kokand for giving protection to other members of Jahangir's family. This enraged Khan Muhammad Amin. He invited Muhammad Yusuf, the elder brother of Jahangir, to retake the throne of Kashgarhia. Yusuf seized Kashgarh. His force also attacted Yarkand in 1830. At this very juncture, complications with Emir Nasrullah Khan (r. 1826-60) of the Emirate of Bukhara compelled Khan Muhammad Amin to withdraw his support to Yusuf. He sent an envoy, Alam Khan, to Peking to make an agreement with the Manchu government. The agreement concluded in 1831 stated that (1) Kokand would levy duties on all imports into Uch Turpan, Aksu, Kashgarh, Yarkand and Khotan and (2) it would appoint *aksakals* (white beards, i.e., elders, consuls) in all the cities of Kashgarhia under a representative to be stationed at Kashgarh and foreigners visiting the cities of Kashgarhia would be subject to their control. Khan Muhammad Amin assured the Manchu government that he would restrain the Khojas.

The Khojas again revolted against the Manchus in 1846. Khoja Khan, the leader of the revolt, styled himself *katta tura*, the great lord. Others—Kichik Khan, Vali Khan, Tavakkul Khan, Sabir Khan, Aktegin Khan and Isa Khan—added *tura* to their names. Khoja Khan and his force first massacred the Chinese merchants of Kashgarh and then resorted to loot, and debauchery. Thus they instilled no respect among the people. When a Manchu force marched towards Kashgarh, Khoja Khan fled to Kokand. The adventure of the Khojas resulted in a human tragedy. The people of Kashgarh, Yarkand and Aksu fearing Manchu reprisal for the acts of the Khojas, fled to Osh in the Khanate of Kokand. Those, who hastened to cross the Terek Pass of the Alai range at night, perished in the snow-drifts.

Vali Khan Tura invaded Kashgarh several times from Kokand in 1855-1857. He set out from Kokand with a force in 1857, and massacred the Manchu posts at Okkalar and Kizil. When he reached Kashgarh, Nur Muhammad, the Aksakal of the Khanate of Kokand, opened the gate of the city to him. Vali Khan Tura killed the Manchu officers and gave their women to his partisans. He enforced the Shariat law strictly, ordering males from six years upward to wear turbans and offer *namaz* in the mosques five times a day. Any breach of this order entailed the punishment of death. He ordered women to wear *hijab**/veil. Its breach by any woman led to her hair being cut. The Manchu government dispatched a large force of Manchu, Badakshani, Balti and others against Vali Khan Tura. When the Manchu force reached the outskirts of Kashgarh, Vali Khan Tura fled to Kokand.

The revolt of the Dungans of Gansu and Shenshi in 1855 had spread to Sinkiang. Most of the Manchu garrisons in Sinkiang had Dungan soldiers. When they heard of the revolt of their brethren, and their killings, they at once avenged themselves on the Hans, whether soldiers or merchants.

After the Manchu takeover of Kashgarhia in 1757-58, the people of Kashgarhia had risen many times against the Manchus on slogans of religion and ethnicity. The uprising of Jahangir in 1820-28 was the principal uprising. The Manchus had always been able to pacify them, although they were then preoccupied with the Opium War (1840-42), the First Anglo-Chinese War, the Westerners knocking at the sea gates, and the Ta'iping Rebellion of the Ta'ping Heavenly Kingdom (1851-64).

China and Russia had no contact with each other in Central Asia before the Russian annexation of the territories of the Kazak, then called Kirgiz, tribes in the reign of Empress Elizabeth (r. 1740-62). The proximity of Manchu and Russian possessions in Central Asia necessitated the settlement of a number of questions. In the context of concessions to the Western powers along the sea coast consequent to the First Anglo-Chinese War, the Russian government requested for similar concessions on its China frontier. The treaty negotiated by I-Shan and Pu-yen-t'ai,

---

* *Hijab* is Arabo-Persian for "veil".

military governor and assistant military governor of Ili, and Kovalevsky at Chuguchak (Chin : T'a-ch'eng), opposite the Russian frontes town of Bakhta on the Ili River, on 25 July 1851 legalized the Russian trade at Kulja/Yining in the Ili Valley and Chuguchak in the Emil Valley.

The proximity of China and Russia in Central Asia also necessitated the definition of their common border. The governments of China and Russia signed a treaty at Peking on 14 November 1860 to demarcate it up to the Uch Bel Pass, assigning the basin of the Naryn River, the upper reaches of the Syr Darya, and Lake Issik Kul in the Tianshan range to Russia. The boundary divided the people—the Kazaks and Kirgizes. The protocol to this treaty signed at Chuguchak on 25 September 1864, assigned the entire region between the Lake Balkash and the Tianshan range to Russia.

The Russian delegation also desired to take the Sarikol region which gave access to the passes that lead from the Pamir knot to the upper Indus River, and Kashmir. The alignment of the western end of the Chinese-Russian border from the Uch Bel Pass to the Pamir knot was the consequence of an Anglo-Russian agreement relating to the Anglo-Russian spheres in the Pamir region and signed in London on 18 September 1895.

The protocol, drawn up in accordance with the terms of the Sino-Russian treaty of 1860, provided the opening of Russian consular and trade centres at Chuguchak and Kashgarh. The treaty of Kulja and the protocol of Chuguchak also allowed Russian merchants access to other frontier towns in Sinkiang. The Russian government, however, did not realize its desire to station a consul at Kashgarh.

Although the government of Tsar Aleksandr II (*b.* 1818; r. 1855-81) signed the protocol of 1864 in the context of Siberia, it also had in mind its interest in Central Asia, where it was penetrating then. The Russian capture of the forts of Tokmak and Pishkek (now Bishkek) in the north Kirgiz region had brought Russia close to the frontier of Sinkiang.

Kashgarhia

Ya'kub Beg, born about 1820 in Pishkent near Tashkent in the Khanate of Kokand, attained high ranks from a *bacha*, "dance boy", in Tashkent to *Emir* (Amir) in Kashgarh, emerging as master of entire Kashgarhia from the Pamilr mountains to Lake Lob nor by 1873. Khudayar Khan (r. 1842-58, 1862-63), after becoming the Khan of the Khanate of Kokand, appointed him *kilaochi*, "fort commander". When fighting between the Khoja factions in Kashgarhia intensified in 1864, Sadik, a Kirgiz chieftain, with the intention to fight back Rashideddin Khoja (Khan Khoja) thought of using another Khoja. He requested Khan Khudayar to send a Khoja to reconcile the Khoja factions. Khan Khudayar sent Buzruk (Buzurg) Khoja, the surviving son of Sayyid Jahangir. Along with him, he sent Yakub Beg as commander with a contingent of soldiers. As the Khan of Kashgarh, Buzruk Khoja appointed Yakub Beg *Batvirbashi*, "Commander-in-chief", of his army.

Jamaleddin Khoja of Aksu did not acknowledge Buzruk Khoja as the Khan of Kashgarh. The armies of Aksu and Kashgarh met at Tuzgun in 1867. Yakub Beg proved his skill as a military strategist. To conceal the strength of his army, he divided it between Buzruk Khan and himself. Although wounded, he won the battle. The people acclaimed him with the title *Bedevlat*, "Fortunate One". He himself assumed the title *Atalik Ghazi*, "Guardian Warrior", and the name of Muhammad Yakub.

Muhammad Yakub sent Yakub Khan Tora as an envoy to Maharaja Ranbir Singh (r. 1857-85) of Jammu and Kashmir in 1871, with the request that the British government in India could be persuaded to enter into a political alliance with him. Maharaja Ranbir Singh supported his request. From Srinagar, Yakub Khan went to Constantinople (Istanbul since 1922). There he agreed to the recitation of the *khutba* in the name of Sultan Abdel Aziz (Abdel Aziz Oglu Mehmet in full, r. 1861-76) of Turkey in the mosques of Kashgarh, i.e. Sultan Abdelaziz as the Khalifa of the Muslims of Kashgarhia. Sultan Abdel Aziz gave Muhammad Yakub the title of *Amir* am-mumin*, "Commander of the Faithful", i.e. Muslims.

Lord Thomas George Baring Northbrook of Stratton, the Viceroy and Governor-General of India (Calcutta) from 1872 to 1876, appointed Thomas. Douglas Forsyth to conduct a mission to Yarkand, Kashgarhia. The staff of native assistants of the Forsyth mission included Nain Singh and Kishan Singh—the surveyor pandits of the Survey of India. Yakub Beg, who was on his way back from Constantinople, accompanied the Forsyth mission. British India and Kashgarhia concluded their treaty of commerce at Kashgarh on 2 February 1874. Queen Victoria (r. 1837-1901) sent a small steam boat to Maharaja Ranbir Singh for his services to the Forsyth mission.

Captain Valikhanov, the adjutant to the Governor General of West Siberia and one of the first Russian agents to visit Kashgarh in 1858, went to Kashgarh disguised as a merchant. Amir Muhammad Yakub's experience of the Russians in his homeland of Kokand had left him deeply suspicious of the Russian motives. Before coming to Kashgarh, he had fought Russian troops at Ak Mesjet in 1853 and at Tashkent in 1864 and had escaped capture with difficulty. He feared

---

* Pronounmced Emir.

that his own as yet unconsolidated position might tempt them to continue their advance into his Kashgarhia. So initially he forbade direct trade with them. But, as he became confident of his position, he sent his nephew Shadi Beg to negotiate with them (Russians) in 1869. General K.P. von Kaufman, the Governor General in Turkestan, was then away in St. Petersburg. So Shadi Beg delivered Amir Muhammad Yakub's letter to General Koplakovsky in Verni (now Almati). Kolpakovsky was not able to negotiate with Shadi Beg. General Kaufman, still in St. Petersburg, asked him to come there.

General Kaufman tried to persuade Khudayar Khan to intervene between him and Amir Muhammad Yakub Khan. Khudayar agreed only to act as a mediator. Kaufman then sent a mission headed by Baron Kaulbars, including an engineer and a topographer, to Kashgarh. At the same time he stationed troops along the route to Fort Naryn on the Naryn River and constructed a road in the border mountains to facilitate military action against Amir Muhammad Yakub if necessary. Amir Muhammad Yakub refused to negotiate with Baron Kaulbars until the Russians halted their military activities on his border. When the Russians did so, the two sides concluded an agreement entitled "Conditions of Free Trade Proposed by General Aide-De-Camp von Kaufman to Yakub Bek" in April-June 1872.

The Kashgarhian-Russian agreement was a reciprocal contract, but difficulties developed soon. General Kaufman sent another mission to Kashgarh, undoubtedly another reconnaissance mission. For, by this time, Kaufman seems to have decided to mount an expedition against Emir Muhammad Yakub.

Russian troops moved into the Ili country of Sinkiang on 4 July 1871 on the understanding that the Russian government would restore it to the Manchu government when it would ensure peace from the insurgency of Emir Muhammad Yakub. The Manchu government appointed General Tso Tsung-t'ang (1812-85), the Governor of Gansu and Shenshi, in 1876 to recover Sinkiang. Tso's expeditionary force first took Urumch'i and Manas in north Sinkiang. Just as the Manchu force crossed the Tianshan range from the north to the south in mid-July 1877, Amir Muhammad Yakub died suddenly, and perhaps unnaturally. The Manchu force under General Liu Ching-t'ang, the second in command of the Manchu expeditionary force, recovered the whole territory of Sinkiang by early 1878. The Manchus pledged non-interference in the religious customs of the Muslims, agreeing to the sanctity of the Shariat in matters of marriages, property and inheritance. The Manchu government organized the entire country from Hami to Kashgarh and from the Irti'sh River to the Pamir mountains with Urumch'i as its capital.

Amir Muhammad Yakub had two sons : Kuki Beg and Hak Kuki Beg. He wished to make the younger son, Hak Kuki Beg, his successor. On the day of the Emir's death in Kurla, Hak Kuki Beg reached there. From Kurla, he set out for Kashgarh, carrying the body of his father. Mehmet Zia Pansat, whom Kuki Beg had deputed to receive Hak Kuki Beg, treacherously slew him. Three persons : Kuki Beg of Kashgarh, Hakim Khan Tura of Uch Turpan and Niyaz Bek of Khotan, claimed the rule of Kashgarhia. Kuki Beg advanced against Hakim Khan, who suffered defeat and fled away. He also defeated the force of Niyaz Bek. He himself escaped to Andijan. His son Mustafa Khan, an employee of the Russian government in Tashkent, visited Kashgarh in 1890 on the plea to claim money from the heirs of Yashur Hakim Beg, the treasure of his grandfather, Amir Muhammad Yakub.

Perhaps the Russian government sent him out to find if the people of Kashgarh would welcome him in the event of the Russian troops moving into Kashgarhia.

Yakub Bek owed his ascendancy to a combination of ethnic and religious factors. To Britain and Russia, motivated by the ambition to advance their imperial interests in Central Asia, he represented both an opportunity and a danger. The British supported him as a barrier against Russian expansion. Amir Muhammad Yakub himself sought to manipulate them, Britain and Russia, to bolster his position against China. A sense of Turkic and Islamic solidarity motivated him to seek the help of Turkey. The response to his overtures to Sultan Abdelaziz was sympathetic, but, owing to distance, it had little effect. Russia shifted its support to China. British support proved inadequate.

Given the political structure of the region, maintenance of Manchu authority in Kashgarhia might have been possible if Peking had not then to put down the rebellions among the Dungans in the intervening territories of in Gansu and Shensi. The course of events in Kashgarhia, however, was not altogether a consequence of the Dungan revolt in Gansu and Shensi. Traditional westward orientation of the people of Kashgarhia had remained strong. The Khojas had strong bases among the Kirgizes and in the Khanate of Kokand. The merchants of the Khanate of Kokand, commonly known as Andijanis, dominated trade in both direction, to and from China. The *tarikat* (fraternity) of the Sufi order and the Andijani merchants, its adherents, were favourably disposed towards the Khojas. The influence of the Andijani merchants provided a basis for a series of attempts by the Khojas to regain Kashgarhia. After the Manchus captured Sayyid Jahangir in 1827, his brother

Muhammad Yusuf continued incursions into Kashgarhia from the Khanate of Kokand. He even sieged the Manchu garrison in Kashgarh for nine months in 1846. Vali Khan Tura, one of the leaders of the Khoja revolt of Muhammad Amin Khoja, held Kashgarh for half a year in 1855. Thus a large number of people in West Turkistan, refugees and direct descendants of those who had fled Kashgarhia in previous decades, had ties with Kashgarhia, which had transcended commercial interests.

China sent Ch'ung Hou to Russia as amassador polenipotenciary in late 1878 to negotiate the return of the Ili country. Russia and China signed a treaty at Livadia in the Crimea on 2 October 1879 to restore the Ili country to China on payment of an indemnity of five million roubles to Russia. The Russian government retained the fertile Tekkes River Valley west of the Khorgos River in order to keep control over the passes through the Tianshan range into South Sinkiang. China also granted other privileges to Russia. When Ch'ung Hou, who had negotiated the treaty, returned to China in late 1879, there was widespread opposition to the terms of this treaty. The Manchu government renounced it on 19 February 1880, deposed Ch'ung Hou and sentenced him to decapitation on 3 March 1880. However, after the renegotiation of the treaty by Tseng Chi-tse, the Chinese minister to Russia since 12 February 1880, the government reprieved him (Ch'ung Hou). By the treaty signed by the Russia and China in St. Petersburg (Chin : San-p'i-t'i-li-p'u-er) on 24 February 1881, Russia returned to China most of the Ili country, including the Tekkes Valley. Peking agreed to pay to St. Petersburg an increased indemnity of nine million metallic roubles. The Manchu government also agreed, in 1882, to Russian consulates at Urumtsi, Guchen,

Hami, Turpan and Kashgarh in addition to those at Chuguchak and Kulja. The first Russian consul to Kashgarh appeared at Kashgarh in November 1882 itself.

The Manchu government formed Sinkiang as a province by an imperial edict on 11 November 1884, naming its capital Ti-hua and General Liu Ching-t'ang the Pacificator its first governor. It ennobled the Uigur leaders of Hami/Komul and Turpan, who had helped in the establishment of Sinkiang, granting them the hereditary title "Beg", Prince. It established Hami/Komul at the eastern end of Sinkiang as a khanate under its suzerainty, leving on it a nominal annual tribute of fresh melons. Hami/Komul has been famous for its melons since ancient times. The Kuomintang (KMT) government annexed a part of easternmost Sinkiang to the province of Qinghai (Ch'inghai) on its formation in the latter 1930s.

Russia had looked towards East Turkistan since the seventeenth century, first calling it "Little Bukhara" to distinguish it from Bukhara proper. East Turkistan acquired special importance for Russia after its troops clashed with Manchu outposts there in the nineteenth century. By the commercial treaty, which the Russian and Manchu governments signed at Kulja on 25 July 1851, Russia obtained the right to establish a consulate at Kulja in the Ili Valley. Russian influence in the Ili country grew strong after its occupation on 4 July 1871. The Sino-Russian treaty, called the Ili treaty of 1881, which restored the Ili country to China, also granted Russia the right of free trade and the right for Russians to buy land and build houses. Russian subjects became free of local jurisdiction. The Sino-Russian treaty of 1881 thus laid the foundation of Russian power in Sinkiang.

Sinkiang of Warlords

The revolution in China on 10 October 1911 spread from Hami to Kashgarh on 24 December, and Sinkiang came under the government of the Republic of China, which Dr Sun Yat-sen (1867-1925) had founded on 1 January 1912. Subsequently, it came under successive warlords. Yuen Wung-fu, the *Taotai* (Commissioner) of Kashgarh and the Governor-designate of the Province, and his wife became victims of the revolutionaries on 7 May 1912. Yang Tseng-hsin of the civil service, the Chief Justice of Sinkiang, became the Governor of the Province in May 1913.

The Bolshevik revolution in Russia posed problems of all sorts to Governor Yang Tseng-hsin. The Turks from West Central Asia and the White Russians sought asylum in Sinkiang (and in Manchuria). The Turk refugees did not pose much problem to Governor Yang. They rehabilitated themselves with their kindred tribes. The Kirgizes nomadized in the pastures on the China side of the Pamir mountains. The rehabilitation of the White Russian refugees (both civilians and soldiers), including the Russian Raskol'niki (Old Believers) and Jews posed much problem to him. So did Admiral Bekich, General Boris V. Annenkov and Ataman Aleksandr C. Dutov of the Orenburg Cossacks and their men. A Soviet agent shot General Dutov in Kulja in 1921. The Yang administration manoeuvred to apprehend General Annenkov in Ti-hua in 1922, eventually passing him on to the Soviet authorities. The Soviets executed him.

After the Sino-Soviet agreement signed in Peking on 31 May 1924, Governor Yang placed the Russian refugees in military, education, agriculture and other services. They moved even to inner China, Hong Kong, India and elsewhere. The Russians even played important roles, crucial at times, in the politics of Sinkiang.

During the rule of Governor Yang, Ti-hua witnessed two gruesome banquet scenes. To the first of those held on 16 February 1916, he invited all whom he suspected of plotting his overthrow. When his guests were drunk and while the band played outside, he had them shot one by one. To the second held on 7 July 1928, it was his turn, along with his officials, to be killed in a burst of bullets by one of his officials—Fan Yao-nan just as a toast was being drunk to the Soviet consul-general, who escaped, along with his wife, to a lavatory. Chin Shu-jen, head of the Political Department of the Province, arrested and executed Fan and supporters.

Chin Shu-jen, who declared himself governor of the Province, faced no easy task when taking over as Governor of the Province. To begin with, he pursued Yang's policy of *modus vivendi*. He even erected a statue of Yang. Then he deviated from it. For example, he confined Maksud Shah, the Khan of Hami/Komul, at Ti-hua. Khan Maksud Shah died in November 1930, and so on. The reforms of Governor Chin led to the Hui rebellion in Hami, overthrowing him on 12 April 1934. He escaped to East China via Siberia. Khoja Niyaz of Komul-Turpan and Sabit Damulla* of Kashgarh and Memet Amin Bugra (1901-65) and his brothers Abdulla and Nur Ahmetjan of Khotan founded the Republic of East Turkistan (RET) at Kashgarh on 1 November 1933, consequent to the intervention of the Huis from Gansu.

The collapse of the Chin regime, and his fall, signalled the transformation of Sinkiang into an exclusively Soviet sphere of interest. The rebels gave General Sheng Shi-tsai the opportunity to seize power. With Soviet help and naturalized White Russian troops, he defeated the rebels. The Soviets helped General

* Turki for *Maulwi*.

Sheng, Governor of Sinkiang since 1933, to crush the RET. The Soviet government had viewed the Republic of East Turkistan as an anti-Soviet Anglo-Japanese creation. It discouraged the governments of Afghanistan and Turkey from taking an active interest in the Republic of East Turkistan. The RET leaders escaped to Afghanistan and India. Memet Amin Bugra wrote a history of East Turkistan in the Uigur language in Kabul and published it in Srinagar. He went to Chungking, the war-time capital of China, in 1945. Khoja Niyaz, as President of the Republic of East Turkistan, had proclaimed it as an Islamic republic.

The Soviet government provided financial assistance to Governor Sheng to enable him to stabilize his position in 1934 and 1937. A Soviet mechanized infantry force, stationed in Hami/Komul since January 1938, ensured Sheng's control over that much-troubled oasis. The Soviet government stationed another military unit in Ti-hua for the security of its aircraft factory there in 1940. This resulted in much amiability between Moscow and Governor Sheng. Sheng even set up a refinery, with Soviet help, to exploit the potential of the Karamai oilfield near Ti-hua.

Sheng Shi-tsai gave the people of Sinkiang an opportunity to express themselves for the first time in the history of the region. The name Uigur for the majority Turki population of the Province began to be used for the first time. Until the time of Sheng, the population of Sinkiang had just been known as Turki. Sheng followed the Soviet example to use the name Uigur for its majority population. He made a secret trip to Moscow in August 1938, especially to discuss Sinkiang with Josep Stalin personally and his own position. He joined the CPSU (Communist Party of the Soviet Union). He even sought membership of the CPC (Communist Party of China). He established

Sinkiang relationships between Moscow, Chongjing (Chungking) and Yen'an. He assigned positions to cadres of the Communist Party of China under terms of cooperation between himself and Yen'an in 1937. He was a pragmatist. He went to Sinkiang in 1930 as a minor staff officer and rose to become its governor. He wrote his memoirs in Chinese in Taipeh, Taiwan

Sheng Shi-tsai broke away from Moscow in the spring of 1944. President Chiang Kai-shek, who needed to improve relations with Moscow then, persuaded Sheng to move from Sinkiang to Chungking on 11 September 1944. He appointed Sheng minister of agriculture and forests. Thereby he also recovered Sinkiang, ousting the USSR from there. General Wu Chung-hsin, Chairman of the Commission of Mongolian and Tibetan Affairs of the Government of China, succeeded Sheng in Sinkiang. General Chang Che-chung replaced General Wu Chung-hsin as Chairman of the Sinkiang provincial government. He was close to Chiang Kai-shek.

Chiang Kai-shek appointed Masut Sabri Chairman of the Sinkiang provincial government in May 1947, but removed him in December 1948. Masut Sabri was the first native governor of Sinkiang. He appointed Burhan Shahidi, also a native of Tatar origin, Chairman of the Sinkiang provincial government. Shahidi had been a civil officer in Governor Yang's administration and Vice-Chairman in Governor Chang Che-chung's administration. Chairman Shahidi and most of the leaders of the Republic of East Turkistan (RET) enabled People's Liberation Army (PLA) to move into Sinkiang in September 1949. The government of the People's Republic of China retained. Shahidi as the Governor of Sinkiang. It moved him to Beijing in 1952. There he became Chairman of the Islamic Association of China, and so on.

After the departure of Sheng from Sinkiang the Kazaks, Uigurs and others, even the White Russians, of the Ili country, had rebelled against the administration of Sinkiang. The Uigur Ahmet Jan Ali Han Tura had led the revolt, locally known as the "Three Districts Revolution". The rebels had proclaimed the Republic of East Turkistan (RET) at Kulja on 12 November 1944. The rebellion of 1944 was anti-Han and anti-Kuomintang. A peace agreement on 6 June 1946 had led to the formation of a coalition government of the republics of China and East Turkistan. Memet Amin Bugra was minister of reconstruction of the coalition government. The coalition had collapsed within a year.

The RET government had continued to govern the three districts of Ili, Chuguchak and Altai (called Ch'eng-hua by the Chinese and Sharasume by the Kazaks) without reference to the Chinese government in Tihua. It ceased to exist when units of the People's Liberation Army (PLA) of the People's Republic of China (PRC) founded by Mao Zedong and associates in Beijing on 1 October 1949 entered into Sinkiang to "liberate" it from the KMT rule. Memet Amin Bugra and others sought asylum in India. They moved to Turkey in 1954, Amin Bugra dieing there in 1965. Except Sepittin, the Minister of Education of the RET government, all its leaders died in a plane crash from Alma Ata to Chungking on 22 August 1949.

Border differences between China and the MPR (Mongolian People's Republic) in the vicinity of the knot of mountains known as the Baitik Bogda/Pei-ta Shan, an outlying spur of the Altai range, north-east of Urumitsi, led to clashes between them. According to the MPR government, the government of the Republic of China provoked the incident of 5 June 1949 in order to slander it to the United Nations, thereby preventing it, the MPR, from acceptance as a member. Initially, the Republic of China had supported the MPR's application for UN membership, but opposed it from 1947 onwards.

The British government of India could not afford to ignore the spread of Soviet influence in Sinkiang. During 1939-40 the administration of Governor Sheng constructed posts, and held them in strength, on the Hunza (Jammu and Kashmir) border facing the approaches to India. All trade between India and Sinkiang ceased. Thousands of Indians, who had been living in Kashgarh, Yarkand and Khotan for generations, had to throw away their British Indian passports because the Sheng administration frowned on those holding them. But Sheng's break with Moscow and Soviet withdrawal from Sinkiang proved favourable to the British government. The KMT government relaxed restrictions on the Hunza border. It even allowed the opening of a postal service between Gilgit and Kashgarh and a British consulate at Urumtsi, the capital of Sinkiang. The British government already had a consulate at Kashgarh.

The Government of the People's Republic of China (PRC) first set about to consolidate the frontier defences of Sinkiang (Xingiang according to the *pinyin* romanization). It eliminated India and the Soviet Union which had been involved there. Soviet advisers and technicians in Xinjiang continued up to 1960 when they withdraw from China. Later (in 1969 and 1974), there were clashes between China and the Soviet Union on the Xinjiang-Kazakhstan border. The 1974 clash became known as the 'helicopter' incident because a Soviet helicopter had landed at Altai in Xinjiang and the Chinese had seized it.

The PRC Government organized Xinjiang as the Xinjiang Uigur Autonomous Region (XUAR) on 1 October 1955 with Saipittin Aziz, a native Uigur, as Chairman. Saipittin had been a member of the CPSU before joining the CPC. The insertion of the word

"Uigur" along with the word "Xinjiang" in the nomenclature of the region was politically satisfying to the Uigurs who had been demanding it since the 1940s. It was recognition of historical reality. The PRC Government also restored the old name Urumtsi (*pinyin* Urumqi)as the capital of the region. As elsewhere in the autonomous regions, it also formed autonomous districts and special administrations in the Kazak Autonomous District (Kulja), the Kizilsu Kirgiz Autonomous District (Artush) on July 1954, and so on. The Ili Kazak Autonomous District comprised the three districts of the former RET.

The PRC Government liquidated or reduced the landlords and rich peasants to peasant status and abolished the existing methods of landownership and irrigation water in the XUAR in 1952-53. It built schools and colleges, universities and academies, theatres, and hospitals, highways, railways and airlines in the XUAR. The language authorities of the People's Republic cyrillized the Arabo-Persian script of the languages of the Uigur, Kazak and other Turks, perhaps to placate the Soviet government, in August 1950, and latinized it in June 1958, when it felt that cyrillization created a bond between them and their fellow Turks in the Soviet Union. The peoples of XUAR resisted the language policy of the PRC Government. Mahmud al-Kashghari had written his *Diwan-i Lugat at-Turk* not only in the Arabic script but also in the Arabic language. This was quite in accord with the spirit of the time, the time of the Arab Khilafat. The Uigur dialect was the first Turkic dialect to be reduced to alphabet writing, its script developing from the Sugdi script. The PRC Government reinstated the Arabo-Persian script in July 1980.

Tsarist or Soviet influence in Xinjiang (Sinkiang) was paramount until 1949. The Tsarist/Soviet government of course never denied China's position there. However, it continued to pressure for concessions in that province right up to its takeover by the Government of the People's Republic of China. Why Xinjiang did not separate from China is interesting. Perhaps the fact that it had been a province and an integral part of China since 1884 constrained the Tsarist/Soviet government from altering its status. Of course, Tsarist/Soviet Russia did not want a strong China to control Xinjiang. Its policy was to exploit China's Far West economically and keep it weak politically. China is strong now, capable of taking care of its interests, and concerns. Like its other constituent parts, XUAR is an integral part of the People's Republic and is in the firm control of its Government.

4

AMU-SYR MESOPOTAMIA

Most of West Central Asia was a part of the Persian empire of the Hakkaman/Achaemen dynasty (B.C. 521-332). The rest was terra incognita. Alexander the Great of Macedon (B.C. 356-323) took Marcanda (later Samarkand), the capital of the Kingdom of Sogd* in the Zarafshan River Valley, in B.C. 328. Afrasiab, the legendary hero of Turan, founded Samarkand 2500 years ago. Alexander founded Alexandria Eschate (the Extreme, Farthest), modern Khojent, besides the Jaxtartes River (modern Syr Darya) on the north-east corner of Markanda. This was the limit of his advance in Central Asia : he did not go north or east beyond it. He married Roksane (Roxana), the beautiful daughter of the Persian King Oxyartes of Bakhtar (Bactria, Chinese: Tattsia). She survived him, bore him a heir.She and her son were killed a dozen years later.

After the advent of Islam in Khurasan, Ibn Muslim Qutaiba (d. 704-715), the vice-roy of Khurasan and commander of the Arab Army, chose Marv (pronounced Merv), the capital of Khurasan, as his headquarters around the 660s A.D. The Arabs killed the last ruler of the Sasan dynasty (226-642),Yazdgard III, in 642. Qutaiba extended the Arab conquests to Bukhara and Samarkand, taking Bukhara in 709 and Samarkand in 712-13. In Bukhara, first his forces met stiff resistance. Eventually, the Regent, Queen mother Qabaj, sued for peace. In Samarkand, he made a treaty with

---

* Sogod of the Arab geographers.

Afshir (Ikhsid)/ King Khurak, respecting Samarkand and its environments. He set up a mosque by converting one of the places of Zoroastrian worship, and stripped the *but* (idols) of the temples of their ornaments. He also took Kashgarh, proceeding from Fargana, in 714-15. Allegedly, he also vowed to take al-Khata, that is, China. A little earth of China upon which Qutaiba might tread to keep his oath, a bag of its money as tribute and four royal youths (on whom he imprinted his seal) released him from his oath—interesting diplomacy adopted by Emperor Chung Tsung of T'ang China.

Shash (medieval and modern Tashkent) and other places came under the *amirs* (governors) of Neshapur in Khurasan of the Arab Khilafat (Caliphate), A.D. 632-1258. They never lived in those places. The Khalifa appointed them for a term and removed them at his pleasure.

Persian Realm

Bukhara emerged as the main centre of power in West Central Asia under Isma'il Saman (b. A.D. 849; r. 872-907) of the Village Saman in Termiz on the north bank of the Amu Darya. Isma'il Saman was a descendant of Bahram Chubin, a Sasan noble of Balkh and general of King Oharmaz IV (r. 579-90) of the Sasan dynasty (226-642). Nasr, his elder brother, was *Amir** of Samarkand then. Ahmad Ibn Isma'il, the father of Isma'il Saman, had been converted to Islam in 819 from the Zoroastrian faith by Asad b. Abdullah al-Qushayri of the Abad tribe and an amir of Khurasan.

Isma'il Saman took Bukhara in 874 and made it his capital. He consolidated the lands of West Central Asia. He built beautiful villas on the plane near Juyi Muliyan. After him, all the amirs of the

* Governor.

Saman dynasty (874-999), altogether nine, held court in Bukhara. The Samani domain extended even over Khurasan, Sistan, etc.

Bilge Kul Kadir Khan, co-Khan of the left or west side of the Karakhan dynasty (940-1125) of Balasagun in the Chu River Valley in the Tianshan range, intervened in Bukhara in the early 990s. He attacked Bukhara of Amir Ab'ul Kasim Nuh II (r. 976-97), seventh amir of the house of Saman, in 992. The Saman dynasty fell because of internal strife.

The fall of Bukhara, the dome of Islam, greatly affected the Sufi Saint Ahmad (*d.*1166) of Yas, later the town of Hazrat-i Turkistan named in his honour. Saint Yasavi wrote on morals in the Turki language. His sermons and treatises, especially his *Divan-i Hikmat*, circulated widely. The Ghaznawis, Karakhanis and Seljuks prevailed in the Samani domain. The Karakhanis transferred their residence to Samarkand in the autumn of 996. Nasr Khan alias Arslan Ilik, the brother of Gur Khan Abu Nasr Ali Ahmad, who succeeded Sutuk Bugra Khan, conquered Bukhara in 999.

The period of the Saman dynasty was the golden epoch of Bukhara—the blossoming of Dari/Persian literature and culture in Central Asia. The poet Abul Hasan Rudaki (884-954), born near Penjikent*, the physician Abu Ali ibn Sina (Avicenna from the Spanish form of his name, 980-1033), born near Bukhara, and Abu Rayhan al-Biruni (973-1048-50), born near Khwarazm (pronounced Khorezm) lived in the period of the Saman dynasty. Rudaki, the greatest poet of the Saman dynasty, was also a singer and harper. He is especially famous for his simple but moving Juyi Muliyan song, which he

* The town of Penjikent abandond in the time of the Arab conquest.

composed and sang in the presence of his patron Amir Nasr II (r. 914-43) of Khurasan. The Juyi Muliyan song affected the Amir so much that he descended from his throne in Herat, bestrode the horse of his sentry and rode off to Bukhara, without stopping enroute, even without putting on his riding boots, and so on.

Abu Ali al-Bal'ami, the minister of Amir Mansur b. Nuh (r. 961-76), translated for him the history of Abu Ja'far Muhammad Tabari (839-923) from Arabic into New Persian in an abridged form in 963. Abu Mansur b. Muwaffaq b. Ali al-Harawi wrote his pharmacologiae for the Samani amir in the New Persian. Poetry, not sciences, flourished under the Samanis.

The Saljuks (pronounced Seljuks), who arose from Dokak Temur Yalig of the Oguz Turk tribe, Western Turks, migrated from Kashgarh of the Karluk Turks to Bukhara. Tugril, (r.1037/38-63), a son of Saljuk, took Marv (modern Mari) on the Lower Murgab River in Khurasan and the title "Sultan" in 1037. He had no offspring. When he died, Alp Arslan (b.1030/1063-72), the son of his brother Chagri (*d.* 1060), succeeded him.

Alp Arslan fought the ruler of the Fatimid Khilafat of Egypt (909-1171) in Damascus in Syria. He extended the Saljuki domain in the territories of Byzantine (Eastern Roman) Empire in the north and west. The battle of Malazgird (Manzikert in present-day Turkey), north-west of Lake Van, between Alp Arslan and Emperor Diogenes Romanus IV (r. 1067-92) of the Byzantime Empire, considered to be a crucial battle in the history of Islam, took place in 1071. He took Jerusalem in 1071. Before his murder in 1072, he had put the Saljuk Empire on firm foundations.

Abu'l Malikshah (*b.* 1052; r. 1072-92), the elder son of Sultan Alp Arslan, succeeded him. He marched into the Karakhan lands, and took Bukhara and Samarkand in 1089. He ran the affairs of his empire with the help of Abu Ali Muhammad b. Ishak, who had been the Nizam al-Mulk, the *vazir/* minister of his father. The Nizam al-Mulk wrote the *Siyasatnama/ Siyar al-Mulk**, "Treatise on State - craft", in simple Persian prose.It is a handbook of state - craft. He recommended consultations with the wise and the aged.

The Nizam al-Mulk built madarsas, called Nizamiya, and observatories in the Saljuk domain. In one of those observatories worked the astronomer Omar Khayyam (1022-1123) of Neshapur (Nishapur on maps). Omar Khayyam, the "Tent Maker", for that is what his name Khayyam means, was aware that the earth rotated on its axis and revolved around the sun.

Muhammad (r. 1105-18), the elder son of Sultan Malikshah, succeeded him. Prince Sanjar (*b.*1092; r. 1118-57), the younger brother and successor of Sultan Muhammad, had governed Neshapur since 1096. The Karakitais (1125-1218) of Balasagun defeated Sultan Sanjar at Samarkand in 1141. Sultan Sanjar fought against the Muslim Oguz tribesmen in 1153. The fight ended in his defeat, the tribesmen capturing him and his wife. Apparently, the Oguz were lenient to him. When his wife died in 1156, he escaped when on a hunting expedition, dying in Marv in 1157. With his death began the fall of the Great Saljuks. Except for the tomb of Sultan Sanjar, the Mongols razed Marv, the metropolis of the Saljuk dynasty, in 1220. The Saljuks had ousted the Persian Buids (r. 932-1085), North-West Persia, from power and restored the authority of the Khilafat in Baghdad in 1055.

---

* Hubert Darke, *The Book of Government* or *Rules for Kings*, London : Routledge and Kegan Paul, 1960 : 2nd edn. 1978.

The infighting among the Saljuks gave rise to Turks in Khorezm. Anush Tegin (*d.* 1097) of Khorezm served in the court of Sultan Malikshah first as cup-bearer and then as governor of Khorezm at Gurgenj Urgench* (Urgenj in Persian) on the lower Amu Darya. Kutbeddin Muhammad Aybek (r. 1097-1127), the son of Anush Tegin and the vassal of the Saljuks, assumed the title "Khwarazm Shah". Atsiz (r. 1127-56), the son of Aybek, tried to rid himself of the Saljuk yoke. The fight between Atsiz and Sanjar ended in Atsiz's defeat. Be that as it may, Sultan Sanjar forgave him and reinstated him. Atsiz again raised the flag of revolt against Sultan Sanjar. The battle between Atsiz and Sanjar again ended in his, Atsiz's, defeat. Sultan Sanjar entrusted Khorezm to his nephew, Sulayman. After Sultan Sanjar's return to Marv, Atsiz captured Urgench again, and overthrow the Saljuks in Khurasan.

Il Arslan (r. 1156-72), the son of Atsiz, succeeded him. Tekesh (r. 1172-1200), the successor of Il Arslan, enlarged the Khorezm realm. Muhammad (r. 1200-20), the second son of Tekesh, defeated the Karakitais in the battle near Taras, and took the western part of their domain in 1210. He was powerful. The frontiers of his domain included Marv, Herat and Balkh. His end came through Chingiz Khan (Chinggis Khan, r. 1205-27), who invaded Khorezm on the plea that several Mongol envoys and hundreds of Muslim merchants, who were with them, had been captured and killed by Gayrkhan Inaljuk, the governor of Otrar, on the charge of spying. Perhaps there were a number of spies among those merchants. At any rate, matters became worse when Muhammad killed the

---

* Capital of ancient Khwarazm, one of the most important cities of Central Asia for centuries.

messengers sent by Chingiz Khan to ask him to hand over the governor of Otrar. This led Chingiz Khan to sweep over Khorezm in 1218, and destroy Urgench in 1221. Chingiz Khan himself led the vast host of his horsemen to Khorezm from the north-east. Muhammad was not in Urgench then.

Muhammad had ignored the logistical counsel of his eldest son Jalaleddin Mankabirni to meet the Mongols at the frontier. He had believed the Mongols would not cross the Amu Darya. He escaped from the troops of Chingiz Khan, who chased him until he died as a fugitive. Jalaleddin defeated the Mongols, the destroyers of Khorezm, in the battle on the Indus River in India in 1221. From there he moved to Khurasan. He died as a fugitive along the coast of the Caspian Sea in 1231. His bravery had astonished even Chingiz Khan. Of course, his courage could not save him from defeat.

The Khorezm domain, like the other contemporary Muslim domains, suffered from family quarrels for power between the Queen Mother Terken Khatun and her son Muhammad or between the father and his son.

Timuri Domain

Temur (1335-1405), commonly known as Timur Lang, Timur the Lame, of the Barlas clan of the Mongol-Turk tribe, born in Village Khoja Ilgar near Kesh (modern Shahri Sabz) on 19 April 1335, consolidated the congeries of the Mongol-Turk entities in West Central Asia. After establishing his supremacy over them, he set himself on the throne of Mawarannahar in 1370. He received the title "Sahib Kiran", the Lord of Auspicious Constilation. He made Samarkand, in the valley of the middle Zarafshan River, his capital. He built the *ark*/fortress in 1371-72. His palace, Kok Saray, was within it. The treasury and prison also were within it. He rebuilt the city wall of Samarkand in 1371-72. He constructed magnificent buildings, drafting masons and craftsmen from Persia and India, and khankahs and laid out beautiful villas there. During his reign Samarkand was the pride of cities, the "face of the earth". Timur also repaired the mausoleum of Hazrat Ahmad Yasavi, the Sultan of the Saints of Central Asia, in Hazrat-i Turkistan.

The domain of (Amir*) Timur extended from Moscow in the north to Delhi in the south and from China in the east to Anatolia in the west. He took Khorezm (modern Khiva) in 1372, and campaigned in Fargana in 1376. His troops captured the wife and daughter of Kamareddin (r. 1365-89) of the Duglat clan, the general of Mogolistan and Khan of Kashgarh. He took Dilshad Aga, Kamareddin's daughter, as his wife in 1379. She died in 1383. He also married Tukel Khanum, a daughter of Sultan Khizr (r. 1389-99) of Mogolistan. He invaded Persia three times, first in 1380, when he subdued Khurasan, Sistan and Mazanderan. He also had relations with Byzantine and France. He died in Otrar on 18 February 1405 crossing the frozen Syr Darya near the mouth of the Arya River, its eastern affluent. He was on his way to conquer China of Emperor Yung Lo (r. 1403-25).

Amir Timur ruled his empire from horseback but according to the *yasa* (*yasak*) of Chingiz Khan. He was the most heroic Central Asia ever produced. Mighty monarchs "crouched", in the words of Christopher Marlowe (the verse dramatist of *Timburlaine The Great*, 1587), "unto his sword". It was certainly courageous of Marlowe, although a non-conformist Christian, to write on the Muslim Timur in the climate of the time—the time of the

* Pronounced Emir.

Crusades. Samuel Taylor Coleridge (Penguin, 1957, p. 286) equated the power of courage of Napoleon with that of Timur.

The remarks of the historian Ibn Khaldun (*Muqaddimah*), who came into contact with him when Damascus, Syria, of the Sultan of Egypt surrendered to him at the end of 1400, are quite instructive. While Sharafuddin Ali Yazdi, the author of the *Zafar Nama*, who wrote for the pleasure of Amir Temur, lauds the praises of his patron, Ahmad ibn Arabshah, the author of the *Adjaib al-Maqdur*, is most scathing of Amir Temur. He calls him "this criminal", "this mad dog". Amir Temur had brought Ibn Arabshah and his mother from Damascus to Samarkand, and educated him. It is interesting to note that Ali Yazdi described only the life and campaigns of Amir Temur, not the political and economic conditions of his regime.

After the death of Amir Temur, his vast empire fell apart due to strife among his discendants—one part passed to his youngest, fourth son Shah Rukh (r. 1405-47), the other to Shah Rukh's first son, Ulug Beg (1394-1449). Amir Temur had designated as his successor Pir Muhammad, his grandson and the son of his eldest son Jahangir (pronounced Jehangir). He had bestowed the kingdom of Khurasan, Sistan and Mazanderan, on Shah Rukh in May 1397. Shah Rukh entrusted the governance of Mawarannahar* to Ulug Beg.

Ulug Beg, who succeeded his father in 1409, had been governor of Mawarannhar during his father's lifetime. He concerned himself with activities such as the establishment of institutions. He was an outstanding astronomer. He constructed

* Arabic for that which lies beyond the river, that is the land beyond the Sayhun (modern Amu) Darya.

his observatory at Samarkand in 1420/21. From this observatory he plotted the coordinates of 1,000 stars on his astronomical tables known as the *Zij-i Ulug Beg* or *Zij-i Jadid-i Sultani* (Royal Almanac) and measured the length of the year. He produced the first map of the heavens. Unfortunately, his end (on 27 October 1449) was tragic : his son Abdul Latif—the tool of religious fanaticism—instigated his death. He was most accomplished of the Timuri rulers.

Abdul Latif, in turn, died at the hands of a certain Baba Husayn in 1450. With his death the house of Amir Temur came to an end in Turkistan.

The Timuris had great interest in poetry and painting and the building of madrasas and observatories. Gauhar Shad, the wife of Sultan Shah Rukh, patronized the founding of the great musalla in Herat and the beautiful mosque in the sacred city of Mashhad (Meshed of maps). The British artillery in the context of the Panjdeh incident in Sarakh in 1885, destroyed it in July-August 1885. The Timuris of India and Khurasan up to the time of Sultan Husayn Baykara (r. 1468-1506) continued the tradition. The period of Emir Temur and his descendants thus was a great epoch in the history of West Central Asia.

Uzbek Khanates

On the disintegration of the realm of Khan Ab'ul Khair (r. 1438-68), a descendant of Shiban*, the Kazaks, Uzbeks and others established their own political domains. The Uzbeks (Ozbeks of the Russian annals) under Khan Abu'l Khair appeared on the north-west frontiers of the Timuri domain in the early years of Ulug Beg's reign. During 1500-1507,

* Shiban was the fifth son of Juchi, the first son of Chingiz Khan.

they spread from the north Caspian steppes to the Amu-Syr region under Muhammad Shibani (Shibek in Persian; *b.* 1449; r. 1499-1510) Khan, the son of Ab'ul Khair. Muhammad Shibani made himself master of Samarkand in the first decade of the 16th century, with Samarkand as his capital. The Turki speaking Uzbeks lorded over the Persian speaking Tajiks. Later, Muhammad Shibani drove the Timuris even out of Khorasan.

The Khanate of Khorezm formed at Urgench (now in Turkmenistan) in 1512. Khiva replaced Urgench as the capital of Khorezm in 1593. The Khanate of Samarkand became the Emirate (Amirate) of Bukhara in 1557. Bukhara. Fargana separated from the Emirate of Bukhara and formed itself as the Khanate of Kokand in 1710. Historically, Andijan had always been the seat of political power in Fargana. Even Zahiruddin Babar (1482-1530), the founder of the Moghul dynasty and empire in India, succeeded his father Umayd Shaykh, on his death, in Andijan at the age of 12 years in June 1494.

The Uzbeks advanced into Khurasan in 1505-06. Khan Shibani, Abu'l Khair's grandson, came into direct conflict with Shah Isma'il (r. 1502-23/24), the founder of the Safavi dynasty (1502-1736) of Persia, over Kirman near Marv. The Persians defeated and killed Khan Shibani in the battle in Tahirabad on 1 or 2 December 1510. The war between the Persians and the Uzbeks continued during the time of Khan Ubaydullah (r. 1510-39/40), the son and successor of Khan Shibani. The Uzbeks defeated the combined forces of Zahiruddin Babar and Shah Isma'il in the battle of Gajdavan, north of Bukhara, on 26 November 1512.

The Uzbek incursions into Khurasan during the time of Tahmasp (r. 1524-76), the eldest son of Shah Isma'il, and Shah Isma'il II (r. 1576-78), the fourth son of Shah Tahmasp, were not so severe. Khan Abdullah II (r. 1551-98) took Bukhara, and made it his capital, in 1557. He assumed the title "Khan" in 1583. He invested Mashhad and sacked it in 1590. He sent envoys to Akbar the Great (r. 1556-1605) to secure his border with India. Khan Abdul Mu'min (1588-99), the only son of Khan Abdullah II, was a weak successor. After his death, his nobles deposed his son Sikander, the last ruler of the Shibani dynasty, and offered the throne to Jani Khan, the husband of one of his daughters. The father of Jani Khan had come to Bukhara Sharif from Astrakhan after its conquest by Tsar Ivan IV (r. 1533-84) of Russia in the 1550s. Jani Khan did not accept the offer. His relative, Baki Muhammad (r. 1899-1600), did in 1599.

Khan Imam Kuli (r. 1611-43) of the Astrakhan dynasty (1599-1785) strengthened the government of Bukhara. During the time of his successor, Khan Abdul Aziz (r. 1645-80), there was fraternal strife in Bukhara. The Khan of Khiva campaigned against Bukhara. Khan Abdul Aziz abdicated in favour of his brother Subhan Kuli. The nobles of Khan Ubaydulla (r. 1702-11) deposed him. Khan Abul Faiz (r. 1711-41) sent a mission to Tsar Peter the Great (r. 1689-1725) in 1716. The Tsar reciprocated by dispatching an embassy to Bukhara in 1717. Khan Abul Faiz lost Balkh to Nadir Shah (r. 1736-47), the Afsar Turk of Persia. A double marriage cemented the treaty between Bukhara and Persia which established the Amu Darya as the border between them. Nadir Shah himself espoused a sister and his nephew a daughter of Khan Abul Faiz.

Nadir Shah took the Uzbek domains on the left bank of the Amu Darya, north of the Hindu Kush. He made his way from Herat to Khiva in 1740 and put Ilbars Khan, the Khan of Khiva, to death. Khan Abu'l Khayr (r. 1716-48) of the *Kishshi Juz* (Little Kazak Division), who dominated Khiva then, had fled Khiva. He was assassinated in 1748.

Mir Ma'sum (r. 1785-1800), the son of Daniyal Khan of the Mangit Uzbek clan and the Atalik of Abu'l Ghazi (r. 1758-85) superceded him. He married a princess of the Astrakhan dynasty. The *Dastur ul-Muluk* of Khoja Samandar reflects the time and life of Bukhara in the 17th century. From 1785 to 1920, there were seven dynasts of the Mangit house of Bukhara : Mir Ma'sum/Shah Mura'd (r. 1785-1800), Mir Hayder (r. 1800-25), Mir Husayn (r. 1825), Nasrullah (r. 1826-60), Muzaffareddin (r.1860-85), Abdul Ahad (r. 1885-1910) and Mir Alam (r. 1910-20). Shah Mura'd took the title "Emir" (Amir).

Mir Ma'sum, as the deputy of Abu'l Ghazi, fought the rebellious Beg of Shahri Sabz and took Karshi. Then he captured Marv, and killed Bahram Ali, the chief of its Kajar Turk tribe. He brought utter ruin on the Marv Oasis by destroying the ancient Sultan Bent dam across the Murgab River south of the city. Even the Mongols of Chingiz Khan, who razed this flourishing city of Khurasan to the ground, had not done that. He transferred the inhabitants of Marv to Bukhara where they continued the silk culture, one of their occupations. Then he invaded Balkh. Timur Shah (r. 1772-93), the second son and successor of Ahmad Shah Durrani (*c.* 1727-73), who had founded the Kingdom of Afghanistan in1747, marched from Kabul against Shah Mura'd. The two sides negotiated peace. Timur Shah and Shah Mura'd never met.

The Uzbek domains in Afghanistan had fallen to Ahmad Shah Durrani without the necessity of his having to campaign there. Before that, Balkh had been Moghul India's border with Central Asia.

On learning of the death of the King of Kabul, Ulug Beg, in 1501, Zahiruddin Babur took it in 1504. It was from Kabul that he had marched on Samarkand and seized it at the end of 1512. But he lost it in 1513 for the third and last time. The campaign of Prince Aurangzeb (1628-1707), the third son of Emperor Shah Jahan (r. 1628-56), in 1646 was the last Moghul attempt to regain Central Asia.

Iltzar Khan (r. 1800-04), the Khan of the Khanate of Khiva, invaded Bukhara in the neighbourhood of Charjui on the left bank of the Amu Darya in the time of Emir Mir Hayder. Muhammad Rahim Khan (r. 1804-25), the son of Iltzar Khan, also marched against the Emirate of Bukhara, and took Marv in 1822.

Mir Husayn, the first son of Emir Mir Hayder (r. 1800-25), succeeded him. He was Emir for three months only. Nasrullah (r. 1826-60), the second son of Emir Hayder, encountered many obstacles in taking the throne at Bukhara-i-Sherif, Bukhara the Noble. He was then the *Beg* (Governor) of the remote Vilayat of Karshi, the cradle of the reigning Mangit dynasty, and took time to reach Samarkand and gain central support. Umar Khan, the paternal uncle of Nasrullah, had taken hold of the rule of the Emirate in the meantime. Even Ayaz Khan, Nasrullah's father-in-law and the *Topchibashi* (War Minister and Commander-in-Chief) of the Emirate, along with its *Kushbegi* (Chief Minister), was in league with Umar Khan. Muhammad Amin (r. 1822-42), the 12-year old son and successor of Umar Khan of the Khanate of Kokand, gave him a friendly reception. Umar Khan also formed an alliance with Khan Allah Kuli (r. 1826-41), the Khan of the Khanate of Khiva.

Emir Nasrullah's reign marked Bukhara's domination of the Khanate of Khiva and triumph over the Khanate of Kokand. Khan Allah Kuli of

Khiva attacked Marv, then under the Emirate of Bukhara. But his successor Rahim Kuli (r. 1841-43) made peace with Emir Nasrullah.

On the eve of the British invasion of Afghanistan, Amir Dost Muhammad fled to Balkh and Bukhara (the British government of India dethroned him on 1 October 1838), along with his second son Muhammad Akbar. He left his family at Balkh with his son Muhammad Afzal, then governor of Afghan Turkistan. Dost Muhammad had formed the province of Afghan Turkistan comprising Kunduz, Andkhui, Maimena and Akcha, known as *char villayat* (four districts), with Balkh as its capital. He returned from Bukhara to Afghanistan after the entry of Muhammad Akbar in Kabul in the night of 1 November 1841.

The troops of the Khanate of Kokand threatened Jizak on the Bukhara-Kokand border—the key to Samarkand from the north. The troops of Bukhara advanced against them, and besieged Oratepe, the border fortress of Kokand, in 1841. The inhabitants of Oratepe massacred the garrison of Bukhara. No sooner did Emir Nasrullah learn of this development, he again sent his troops to Oratepe. Khan Muhammad Amin again retreated. This time the Bukhara troops chased him up to the capital of his Khanate, Kokand. The peace, concluded at Kohna Badam, bound Khan Muhammad Amin to cede Khojent and other frontier towns to Bukhara. Emir Nasrullah made Sultan Mahmud, the brother and rival of Khan Muhammad Amin, who had fled to Bukhara, the Beg of Oratepe. However, the two brothers, Muhammad Amin and Sultan Mahmud, reconciled. A force of Bukhara captured Khan Muhammad Amin near Margelan and executed him, along with his brother Sultan Mahmud and two sons and relatives, in his own capital in the winter of 1841-42. Emir Nasrullah also ordered the poetess wife Nadira of Khan Muhammad Amin to be hanged. She had composed verses on the hard lot of the women of Central Asia.

Later, Musliman Kul, the chief of the Kipchaks of Namangan took the capital Kokand, captured the Bukhara garrison and set on the throne Shir Ali (r. 1842-45), a son of Khan Muhammad Amin. A force of Bukhara under Khudayar Khan, a grandson of Khan Muhammad Amin and a pretender to the throne of the Khanate, appeared before the capital Kokand. However, Khudayar Khan reconciled himself with Musliman Kul and turned against Emir Nasrullah. A Bukhara force under Shahrukh Khan, the Topchibashi, marched against the Khanate of Kokand. Shahrukh Khan had not advanced beyond Oratepe, when Emir Nasrullah fell ill at Samarkand on 11 October 1858. Emir Nasrullah died in Bukhara Sharif in 1860.

Emir Nasrullah consolidated the state power of Bukhara. He created the *sarbaz* (infantry), the first regular army of the Emirate. He used it in his campaign against Shahri Sabz and Kokand in the 1840s. He constructed Zindan, the state prison in the *ark*, the citadel in the middle of Bukhara Sharif. He confined Lieutenant-Colonel Charles Stoddart and Captain Arthur Conolly of the Indian Army to rigorous imprisonment prior to their public execution on 24 June 1842. John MacNeill, the British minister at the Persian court, had sent them to Bukhara Sharif as spies in 1838 and 1841 respectively. He had sent Col. Stoddart on the retirement of the Persian army from Herat in the summer of 1838. When Emir Nasrullah learnt of the revolt against the British force at Kabul in 1841, he also dismissed the Russian embassy of Col. Butanev.

Muzaffereddin (*b.* 1823, r. 1860-85), the eldest son and *katta tura** of Emir Nasrullah, succeeded him. He had been the Beg of Karshi for one year and of Kermineh for eighteen years. Jirabek, the nephew (sister's son) of Muzaffereddin and Beg of Shahrisabz had contested the succession.

Emir Muzaffereddin began by resuming his father's campaign against Shahrisabz, and Kokand. The affairs in the Khanate of Kokand had taken a new turn. While Khan Khudayar (r. 1862-63, 1871-75) was campaigning against the Russians, his elder half-brother Mallya had been named Khan of the Khanate. The Beg of Oratepe, a native of Shahrisabz, had allied himself with Mallya. Khudayar, who had small forces to oppose those of Mallya, fled to Bukhara Sharif in 1863. The Kipchaks assassinated Mallya and proclaimed Shah Murad Beg, the son of Khudayar's elder brother Sarimsak as the Khan of the Khanate. Shah Murad ruled until the return of Khudayar from Bukhara Sharif-Slighted as the protector and son-in-law of Khan Khudayar, Emir Muzaffer attacked Kokand in April 1863. The peace settlement divided the Khanate of Kokand into two parts : the capital Kokand to Shah Murad and Khojent to Khudayar.

Abdur Rahman Khan, the son of Afzal Khan and a grandson of Amir Dost Muhammad of Afghanistan, fled to Bukhara, when Shir Ali Khan, the eldest son and heir-designate of Amir Dost Muhammad succeeded his father in 1863. With the countenance of his father-in-law, Emir Muzaffer, he crossed the Amu Darya. He entered Kabul on 1 March 1866, expelled Shir Ali from power and transferred it to his father, Afzal Khan, who died next year. Shir Ali

* *katta tura* is Turki for "heir-apparent".

had imprisoned Afzal Khan and Azam Khan, his half-brothers, who had ruled north of the Hindu Kush and had revolted against him. In mid-1869, Abdur Rahman Khan again sought refuge in Bukhara, and Samarkand, which had by then become part of Russian Turkestan. General K.P. von Kaufman, Governor-General of Turkestan, had taken it from Bukhara on 14 May 1868. General Kaufman gave Abdur Rahman Khan a stipend but did not encourage him to disturb the Afghanistan-Bukhara border. Abdur Rahman Khan returned to Afghanistan in 1880 to become Amir of Afghanistan with British support.

The war between Bukhara and Russia had broken out over the Khanate of Kokand, the vassal of Bukhara. Jizak, the frontier outpost of the Emirate of Bukhara, first turned back the Russian advance in the Hungry Steppe in the region of Samarkand. Bukhara suffered its first defeat at Irjai on the left bank of the Syr Darya between Jizak and Khojent on 20 May 1866. General Kaufman captured Samarkand on 1 May 1868. Emir Muzaffer accepted the former's terms. He had unavailingly sought to forge alliances with his neighbours—Afghanistan and Khiva—against Russia. When even Britain declined his appeal for help (—this was the time of the policy of "masterly inactivity" of Lord John Lawrence, Viceroy and Governor-General of India from 1864 to 1869), he had no option but to conclude peace with General Kaufman. Alone, and by himself, he could not resist General Kaufman.

The peace terms between Russia and Bukhara ceded Samarkand and the adjacent territories to Russia, and allowed the government of Tsar Aleksandr II (r. 1855-81) to establish cantonments at Kermineh, Karshi and Charjui. The terms also provided for mutual free trade. The Emir allowed the Russians even to maintain trade agents in Bukhara Sharif and the other towns of the Emirate.

Bukhara and Russia delimited their common border in the following year. By another treaty between Russia and Bukhara concluded on 28 September 1873, the Russian government transferred to the Emirate all the territories of the Khanate of Khiva on the east bank of the Amu Darya. After the Emirate came under the suzerainty of Russia, its borders with Afghanistan and Persia remained constant, and stable.

The nineteen-year old Abdul Malek Khan and his supporters such as Jirabek and Bababek of Shahrisabz did not like the settlement with General Kaufman. He raised the standard of revolt against his father, Emir Muzaffer. The Emir appealed to the Russian government for help against his son's revolt. Russian forces defeated Abdul Malek Khan and captured Karshi on 21-23 October 1868. Jirabek and Bababek escaped to Kokand. Khan Khudayar Khan betrayed them to the Russians.

The Bukhara-Russia treaty of 1868 preserved Bukhara juridically sovereign with its own political and economic systems, though with much diminished territories. The Emir continued to rule the country autocratically. Even the establishment of the Russian political agency in Kagan, Bukhara Sharif, on 12 November 1885 with Colonel Nikolai Charikov as the first Russion resident agent, left the Emir as ever. Charikov was then diplomatic attache at Tashkant. He served up to 1889. He had belonged to the Central Asian section of the Aziaskii Parikaz (Asiatic Department) of the Peselky Parikaz (Foreign Office) of Russia. He recounted his time at Bukhara in his book, *Glimpses of High Politics* (London, 1931). The establishment of the Russian political agency and the appointment of the Russian political agent completed the process of the Russian protectorate over the Emirate of Bukhara, and transformed Bukhara-Russan relations.

Up to the establishment of Russian power in West Central Asia in the 1860s, there was constant warfare between Bukhara and Khiva and between Bukhara and Kokand. The Russian government preserved the Emirate of Bukhara and the Khanate of Khiva, in truncated form of course, as vassal states, but it absorbed the Khanate of Kokand in its Turkestan in1876. The conflict between Bukhara and Kokand had facilitated the advance of Russia into Central Asia. The Khanates of Bukhara, Khiva and Kokand had, possessed then the Mesopotamia of the Amu and Syr Rivers.*

During the time of Emir Abdul Ahad (*b.* 1859; r. 1885-1910), the fifth and youngest son of Emir Muzaffer, there arose a revolutionary movement in Bukhara Sharif under the glow of the first revolution in Russia in 1905-07 and through the stimulus of the Persian and Turkish revolutions of 1906 and 1908 respectively. Ahmad Donish (1827-97) of Bukhara Sharif had criticized feudal backwardness of the Emirate and had advocated the reorganization of its political system. The revolutionaries of Bukhara Sharif sought to oust the Mangit dynasty, and modernize the country. This first revolutionary movement in Bukhara however failed to take root. The revolutionary ferment in the centre of the Russian empire had reached Bukhara Sharif through the Muslim reformists of the Caucasus and Crimea. Mir Said Alam (r. 1910-20), the son and heir-apparent of Emir Abdul Ahad, steered a middle course between the *Qadimi* conservatives and the *Jadidi* progressives for the first few years of his reign.

The movement *Jadidism* in Bukhara Sharif developed from a movement advocating reform of

---

* The Oxus and Jaxartes of the Greeks and the Sihun and Jihun of the Arabs. *Oxus* is from *Vaksha* of the Sanskrit tradition.

the systems of administration and education to a movement advocating reform of the system of politics. The Jadids of Bukhara Sharif had also demanded the establishment of a proper economic system. They had also dreamt of a constitution similar to that of the Young Turks of Turkey. The cultural activity of the Jadids of Bukhara Sharif had met with the resistance of even the masses who were under the sway of the mullas. On 18 July 1914, Emir Mir Said Alam closed all "new schools". The rallying point for anything forward-looking in Bukhara, the few "new schools", which had managed to survive, had played a significant role in forging the leadership of the impending revolution in the Emirate. Mulla Jorabai had opened the first "new school" in Bukhara Sharif in 1900.

The overthrow of Tsar Nikolai II (r. 1893-1917) and the establishment of the provisional government of Duma (Parliament) in Petrograd (the name of the Russian) capital had been changed to Petrograd in the first year of the World War) on 11 March 1917 brought the Jadids of Bukhara Sharif into the open. In response to a congratulatory telegram from the Jadids, the provisional government sent a dispatch to A.Y. Miller, the representative of the erstwhile Russian government in Bukhara, and to Emir Said Alam urging reform. The provisional government, too busy with its own problems of continuning the imperialist war and countering the second wave of revolutionary activity, paid no further heed to Bukhara. So preoccupied was it with the task of stopping the advance of Bolshevism that, except for renaming the designation from political agent to resident, it did not appoint its own representative at Bukhara Sharif. It retained in that post Miller, the erstwhile Tsarist agent who seems to have co-operated with Emir Said Alam. But the clamour for reform was so great that Miller had no alternative but persuade the Emir to issue a manifesto of reforms on 7 April 1917.

The Manifesto, pledging fiscal, judicial and educational reforms and representative government for the capital city of the Emirate, satisfied none. The Emir, on the other hand, repealed the reforms and arrested the revolutionary leaders. The Russian workers in Kagan Novaya Bukhara, New Bukhara, the railway station near Bukhara Sharif, protested. Frightened by the alliance between the revolutionaries of the Emirate and the Russian workers, the Emir released the revolutionaries. He broke off relations with Petrogard, negotiated with the Russian Whites, the British intelligence agents in Kashgarh (Sinkiang) and Mashhad (Persia) and Amir Amanullah (r. 1919-29) of Afghanistan and took measures to stop the growth of revolutionary sentiment in the Emirate. The great advantage he had over the radicals was the exceedingly thin proletarian stratum in Bukhara, and not only in Bukhara but in entire Central Asia.

The Young Bukharan Party* of the Young Bukhara movement was too weak to overthrow Emir Alam by itself. It sought help from the government of the Tashkent Soviet, later the Autonomous Soviet Republic of Turkestan, which the Russian Bolshevik and railway workers had formed on 12 September 1917. F. Kolesov, the Chairman of the Council of People's Commissars of the Tashkent Soviet, promised to help the Young Bukharan Party. But owing to unforeseen development, he was unable to provide the promised help. Just when the Young Bukharan Party was to start its armed struggle in

---

* The radical Bukharans, a part of the Jadids, had separated from them in 1916.

the Emirate with Kolesov's help, two events, besides other hurdles, happened : the loss of connection with the central authority in Petrograd via Orenburg and the proclamation of a provisional government of an autonomous Turkistan in Kokand on 22 December 1917. Mustafa Chokai Oglu (Mustafa Chokaiev, 1890-1938) of the provisional government of autonomous Turkistan sought help from Ataman Aleksandr Dutov, who ordered Cossack detachments in Orenburg to help the counter-revolution in Kokand.

After Kolesov's Red Guards smashed the army of autonomous Turkistan on 18 February 1918 (-Mustafa Chokaiev escaped), Kolesov turned his attention to Bukhara, which, with the influx of the Whites from Kokand and elsewhere into Bukhara Sharif, was turning it into a spot of anti-Soviet activity. Kolesov and Faizullah Khoja (Faizullah Khojaev, 1896-1938), the son of a wealthy merchant of Bukhara Sharif and Chairman of the Young Bukharan Party, demanded reforms to be put into immediate effect by a body elected from the Young Bokharan Party and headed by the Emir himself. The Emir hedged for time. Kolesov refused to wait. He ordered his troops, accompanied by the Young Bukharans, to advance on the city on 1 March 1918. The Emir issued another manifesto, more libreal than the first, conceding the demands of the revolutionaries.

Kolesov and the Young Bukharans also demanded the disarming of the Emir's forces. The Emir demurred, saying that while he personally would be happy to fulfil this demand, his soldiers (and the mullas) were so aroused that it would be difficult to persuade them to lay down their arms. He asked for three days in which to disarm. Kolesov reduced it to twenty-four hours. While Kolesov and the Young Bukharans waited in Kagan for news from Bukhara Sharif, the Emir reorganized his forces. He declared *Jehad* (*Jihad*, holy war) and surrounded the revolutionaries. The revolutionaries had the advantage of artillery, cannon and machine guns. But this seemed to work against them. Ammunition being almost exhausted, Kolesov retreated through dreadful conditions, barely escaping with his life and a part of his force.

Emir Alim, although bereft of moral confidence, resolved to repress the slightest sign of disaffection in Bukhara. He financed the counter-revolutionary Basmach rebellion, which had begun in Farghana in 1918, and struck up an alliance with Amir Amanullah of Afghanistan, who presented him, Emir Alim, several cannon. Amir Amanullah perhaps cherished the hope of uniting the various Muslim elements under the banner of Pan Islam, carried by Afghanistan, into a Central Asian Islamic state. Whether or not Amir Amanullah entertained such grandiose hope is difficult to say. He was, however, cautious in his policy : while helping Emir Alim materially, he took care not to antagonize the Soviets.

A conference of the Young Bukharan Party, held in Charjui on 18 August 1920, decided on an armed uprising in the Emirate, supported by Russian railway workers of Charjui. It addressed an appeal to the government, the proletariat and the Red Army of Soviet Russia, wherein, speaking in the name of the people of Bukhara, it requested for help in its struggle against the Emir. On 28 August 1920, General M.V. Frunze, Commander of the Red Forces on the Turkestan front, ordered his troops to help the Young Bukharan Party. On 31 August, excepting the heir and two other sons. Emir Alim along with his entourage escaped to Dushanbe in Upper Bukhara and Afghanistan, and, eventually, to Europe. He continued to encourage resistance in Bukhara from Afghanistan through the Basmach counter-revolutionaries. His presence in Afghanistan made Amir Amanullah apprehensive of the danger of the Soviet advance towards his borders. Amir Amanullah supported him, but he also cultivated relations with the Soviet government. Actually, he was among the first to recognize Soviet Russia. Emir Said Alam (*d.* 1944) wrote his memoirs *La voix de la Bukharie opprimee* (Paris, 1929) in French.

The Young Bukharan Party organized the revolutionary committee and the Soviet of People's Commissars in Bukhara Sharif. The *kurilatai* (assembly) of the representatives of the people of Bukhara held on 14 September deposed Emir Said Alam and proclaimed the Bukhara Khalkh Shorlar Jumhuriyati (Bukhara People's Soviet Republic). The Soviet government recognized it on 6 November 1920, and abrogated all treaties and agreements concluded with the Emir of Bukhara by the Tsarist government. Thus disappeared the Emirate of Bukara from the map of West Central Asia.

Khanate of Khiva

Ilbars, a scion of the Shibani house, came to power in Khorezm, hence forward called by the name of its capital Khiva. Abu'l Ghazi Bahadur Khan (r. 1644-63) advanced to the vicinity of Bukhara. He wrote *Shejarat at-Turk* in Chagatai Turki. Anusha Khan (r. 1663-87), his son and successor, was also powerful. Khan Shah Niyaz sought the help of Tsar Peter against Bukhara in 1700. The son and successor of Khan Shah Niyaz crushed the Russian expedition of Prince Bekovich Cherkaski, the former Khoja Nefes, in 1717. Khan Ab'ul Khair (r. 1716-48) of the Little Kazak Division, who dominated the Khanate of Khiva then, fled on the advance of Nadir Shah of Persia in 1740.

The Kongrat Uzbek family established the Kongrat dynasty of Khiva and assumed the title "Khan"in 1804.

The Turkmen tribes of the Khanate of Khiva revolted from 1856 to 1865. Russia conquered the Khanate of Khiva on 2 June 1873. General Kaufman himself led the Russian expedition to Khiva. The treaty of peace signed by Russia and Khiva at Khiva on 25 August 1873 fixed the border between the Khivan and Russian territories. It ceded to Russia all the Khivan territory on the right bank of the Amu Darya, along with all sedentary and nomadic inhabitants. The terms also established free mutual trade between Khiva and Russia, and so on. Khan Muhammad Rahim (r. 1865-1910) retained his sovereignty but had to renounce direct dealings with his neighbouring sovereigns and khans. The age-old way of life in the Khanate continued.

Khan Isfandiyar (r. 1910-18) proclaimed modernization and social reforms. He visited Moscow and St. Petersburg. There was Turkmen resistance during 1912-15. Junayt Khan (1860-1938), born as Kurban Memet, of the Junayt clan of the Yomut Turkmen tribe had led the Turkmens since 1914. He met with serious reverses in 1916 and fled first to the Karakum Desert and then to Persia and Afghanistan. He returned to Khiva, and acceded to power, in September 1917.

Establishment of the Provisional Government in Petrograd in February 1917 encouraged the Young Khivans to seek political and other reforms in the Khanate. They came out in the open in most towns of the Khanate and demanded the setting up of a *majlis* (assembly). This frightened Khan Isfandiyar and he agreed to it on 5 April 1917. But he reneged soon and arrested most of the Young Khivan leaders. The others fled. They established a bureau in Tashkent, and captured the capital city, Khiva, of the Khanate in 1918. Junayt Khan escaped from the capital when the Young Khivans proclaimed the Khorezm People's Soviet Republic (KPSR) in February 1920, Khan Muhammad Rahim (r. 1918-20) escaped to Afghanistan.

Khanate of Kokand

Shah Rukh of the Mangit clan of the Uzbek tribe founded the Khanate of Kokand in 1798. His son, Alam Khan (r. 1799-1812), built the capital city, Kokand, of the Khanate in 1810. The Kokandis constructed Ak Mesjet in the Kazak steppes in the time of Alam Khan. Khan Muhammad Amin (r. 1822-42) tried to check the advance of Russia into Central Asia. His troops surprised a detachment of the Cossaks of Orenburg, which had gone round the town of Hazrat-i Turkistan from the right bank of the Syr Darya, for the first time in 1838. He wielded much influence even in the politics of Kashgarhia. His end came through his involvement with Emir Nasrullah of the Emirate of Bukhara.

The Khanate of Kokand was important to Russia in the Pamir context. A Russian expeditionary force under General Kaufman took it in 1876. On 20 March 1876 Tsar Alaksandr II sanctioned its annexation to Russian Turkestan under its ancient name Farghana and appointed. Mikhail Dmitriavich Skobelev, an ardent soldier of the campaign, became its first governor.

The forging of political, military and economic alliance on 4 March 1921 between the governments of the Bukhara People's Soviet Republic (BPSR) and the Russian Soviet Federative Socialist Republic (RSFSR), along with that between the governments of the Khorezm People's Soviet Republic (KPSR) and the RSFSR, initiated a new era in the history of West Central Asia.

5

RUSSO-SOVIET STRAPY

The contacts of the Slavs, the Russians, with the peoples of Central Asia trace to ancient times. Throughout early history, the Russians kept themselves in contact with cultures whose roots were wholly or partially in Central Asia. Contacts between them and Khorezm, a leading centre of ancient Central Asia, trace to AD 860, the year of the founding of the Russian state of Moscovy by Rurik.

Russia first began to advance towards Asia in the middle of the 16the century. The forces of Tsar Ivan IV* (1530-84), Grozny/Terrible, took the Tatar Muslim *khanates* (domains of khans)—Kazan of Khan Yadigar Muhammad on the bend of the Atil (Itil) River, the Middle Volga, at the confluence of the Kama River on 2 October 1552 and Astrakhan/Haji Tarkan** of the Nogai Khan Yagurchai (Yamgurchai, r. 1544-56) on the estuary of the Volga in 1556. Kazan and Astrakhan, along with the Khanate of the Krim/Crimea, had been the successor states of the Dasht-i Kipchak*** of Jochi (*c.* 1176-1227), the eldest son of Chingiz Khan. The conquest of Kazan opened the way for Russia to expand eastward to the Ural range, highest altitude only 550 feet above the level of the sea. The Khanate

---

* Ivan IV, when he took the crown at Moscow in 1547, had taken the title *Tsar*. Tsar Pater (1672-1725) adopted the title Tsar of All Russias that is Emperor, in 1721.

** An Altaic term; rank of nobility. Tsar Ivan IV absorbed Astrakhan in Russia in 1556-57.

*** *Dast-i Kipchak* of the Muslim authors and *Zolotaya Orda*, "Golden Horde", of the Russian annals.

of Kazan had been founded by the Mongol Khan Ulug Muhammad in 1437.

The Volga River, the great waterway from Central Russia to the Caspian Sea, facilitated Russia's advance southwards, and opened the route to the leading centres of Russia such as Nizhnii Novgorod/Nizhegorod (now Gorky). Traders from Central Asia, Persia and India, even from East Asia, attended the fair of Novgorod in the late summer. Russian traders used Astrakhan as a base from which to trade with Central Asia. Tsar Ivan IV granted a concession of salt and mining in the Kama River Valley, the Ural range of mountains and all lands east of the Ural range to the Stroganov family of Novgorod origin, entrusting to it the guarding of the eastern border of his empire.

The Russian Cossaks crossed the Urals eastward into Siberia/Sibir/Shivir in the 1550s. According to a saying, Russia's slope was to the east. Yermak (*d.* 1584) and his band captured Sibir, the capital of the Khanate of Sibir of Khan Yedigir, on the Irtish River in 1581. Khan Yedigir became a vassal of Tsar Ivan IV. Later Khan Kuch'um (*c.* 1563-98) broke this vassal relationship with Russia. This led to the abolition of the Khanate of Sibir. Yermak was in the employ of the Stroganov family to defend their holdings and explore west of the Urals. The Cossaks ultimately marched across Siberia, taking territories of the native tribes and building fortified Cossak settlements and reaching the Amur River and the Pacific Ocean by 1639.

This brought the Russians in close proximity, and conflict, with the Manchus, who had established themselves in China in 1644. China and Russia concluded treaties such as the treaty signed at Nerchinsk (Chinese : Ni-pu-ch'u) on the Nercha River on 29 August 1689. The Chinese-Russian treaty of

1689, the first treaty China ever signed with a Western state, was favourable to China. It limited Russian expansion to the Amur River. The Amur River and the Great Khingan Mountain range then formed the boundary between the Manchu and Russian empires. This treaty between China and Russia, however, did not relate to Central Asia. The treaty, which China and Russia signed at Chuguchak (Chin : T'a-ch'eng) on 25 July 1851 was also in the context of the Russian position in Siberia. But it laid the first foundation of the penetration of Russia from its part of Central Asia into Sinkiang, China.

The government of Empress Anna Ivanovna (*b.* 1693; r. 1730-40) founded the town of Orenburg, east of the Urals, at the junction of Central Asia and Siberia in 1732. Along with the fortress of Orsk, Orenburg was the most important fortress on the eastern frontier of Russia. It became a strong civil and military centre in course of time. Under Neplyuyev, the governor of Orenburg, Russian forces pushed up the Syr Darya to the Karatau range. Khan Abu'l Khair of the Western *Kishshi Juz* (Little Division) swore an oath of loyalty to Empress Anna Ivanovna in 1731. Khan Ablai Membet of the *Orta Juz* (Middle Division) swore his loyalty to her in 1740. Khan Ablai of the Eastern *Ulu Juz* (Great Division) submitted to Russia in 1742-47. The Orenburg administration abolished the Khanate of the Orta Juz in 1822. To deal with Central Asian affairs, the Russian government established the Asia Department in its Foreign Office in 1824.

Russian troops founded along the fringe of the southern Kazak steppes a line of forts. They founded Fort Vernii (Vernoye) on the site of the old Kirgiz city of Almati (Alma Ata since 1929, Almati since 1992) on the Almati River between Lakes Balkash and Issikul in 1854. Before that, although the territories of the Cossaks of Siberia and the Kazaks of the steppes had bordered, there does not seem to have been much intercourse between them. The Chinese-Russian treaties had been mostly in the context of the Mongol and Tungus tribes on the Chinese-Russian borders.

The Cossaks, who had built forts in Omsk in 1716 and Semiplatinsk*, the old capital of the Oirat Mongols in 1718, and so on, established their first post on the Syr Darya in 1847. They took the fortress of Ak Mesjet of the Khanate of Kokand and renamed it Fort Perovsk on 27 July 1853. Russian advance across the Kazak steppes during the reign of Tsar Nikolai (r. 1835-55) brought it in contact with the Khanates of Khiva and Kokand. The Cossaks took the fortress of Suzak of the Khanate of Kokand, north-east of the town of Hazret-i Turkistan, in 1854. The administration of General A.P. Bezak, the Governor-General of Orenburg, set up civil and military centres up the Syr Darya. It took the territories between the Aral and Caspian Seas up to 1863. It captured Hazret-i Turkistan and Auli Ata on 16 June 1864, and Chimkent on 2 October 1864. It captured Tashkent on 29 June 1865. Mulla Alamkul, the Kipchak chief, died in battle with the Russians in the vicinity of Tashkent on 21 May 1865. Russia had occupied all the plains between the Syr Darya and Amu Darya up to 1869.

The Orenburg administration had also formed the small Aral Sea Flotilla of steamers and launches in the 1850s, disbanded after the formation of the Amu Darya Flotilla on 13 November 1887.

Emir Abdullah Mu'min (r. 1557-98) of the Emirate of Bukhara sent an embassy to Tsar Fyodor Ivanovich

* Russian for seven Buddhist monasteries of the Oirat Mongols on the Irtish River.

(r. 1584-98), the son of Tsar Ivan IV, in 1589. Tsar Fyodor Ivanovich reciprocated it. Consequently, a trade intercourse developed between Bukhara and Russia. The merchants of Bukhara, like the merchants of the other Uzbek khanates, carried their merchandise to Astrakhan and Kazan and visited the fairs in Novgorod in Central Russia and Orenburg, Kiziljar/Petropavlosk and Troitsk on the border of West Siberia. Muslim merchants from the Central Asian khanates had traded at the Novgorod fair since the fourteenth century.

The Uzbek khanates sent embassies to Tsar Ivan to ask for a "free" road. Commerce was the major concern of the Uzbek embassies to Russia in the sixteenth-seventeenth centuries. Russia had reciprocated even though Russian merchants themselves had not traded directly with Central Asia then : Indian and Muslim merchants of Astrakhan had acted as agents of Russian trading houses.

Peter the Great (r.1689-1725) was the first Tsar of All Russias to begin the Russian expansion in Central Asia. Khan Shah Niyaz, the Khan of Khiva, had sought the help of Tsar Peter for protection against his rivals in 1700. Tsar Peter dispatched embassies to Persia of Shah Sultan Husayn (r. 1694-1722) and Khiva in 1708 and 1717 with the aim of opening a trade route to India by way of the Caspian Sea. He dispatched an embassy under Prince Tserkaski to Khiva in 1716, killed in Khiva in 1717. The Russians thus associate their awareness of the Eastern World with Tsar Peter the Great. Tsar Peter even stimulated interest in oriental, especially Islamic, studies. He set up a school for the study of Eastern languages in 1702, and arranged for the first translation of the *Kura'n* in Russian. The study of the Eastern World, initiated first by the Russian Ecclesiastical Mission in Peking in the second decade of the eighteenth century and then by the Religious Academy in Kazan in the middle of the nineteenth century, led to the establishment of the Imperial Oriental Institute in 1900.

Availing himself of the chaos in Persia then, Tsar Peter captured the Persian possessions such as Gilan, south of the Caspian Sea. Russia and Persia signed their first ever treaty at St Petersburg on 23 September 1723. Tsar Peter agreed to help Shah Tahmasp II* (*r.* 1722-32) of Persia against the Afghans in lieu of the cession by Persia to Russia of the cities of Baku and Derbent on the Caspian, and Asterabad (modern Gurgan) on the eastern corner of the Caspian. The government of Empress Anna Ivanovna returned its Persian possessions to the Persian government in 1735.

The successors of Tsar Peter had the same aim. The Central Asia policy of Empress Kathrin (Catherine the Great, r. 1762-96) was to establish a frontier from which to conduct trade with Bukhara and the other khanates of Central Asia. By her *ukase* of 9 May 1780, she permitted Sunni Muslim pilgrims from Central Asia to Makka (Mecca) to cross Muslim lands held by Russia. These pilgrims could not travel to Makka through the most direct route across Shii Persia. By an ukase in 1788, she established the Religious Council of Muslims at Ufa. She also countenanced the Russian desire to build a madrasa, a theological school, in Bukharai Sharif.

The Russian policy had not passed unnoticed in Central Asia itself. The khans and people were well

---

* Shah Tahmasp (r. 1525-76) of the Safavi dynasty (1502-1736). Shah Tahmasp II deposed by his General Nadir Kuli, subsequently known as Nadir Shah, in 1730 and killed by Rizakuli, the son of Nadir Shah, in 1739.

** decree akase is Russian for imperial

aware of the danger of Russian expansion. The merchants, who had long resided in Russia, extolled the spirit of Russian justice and order even though they also had the same detestation for anything that was not Muslim. Russian conquest of Geogria in the Caucasus/Kohkaf/Kavkaz mountains in the time of Empress Catherine the Great in 1796 caused great anxiety to the Persian and Turkish governments. Emperor Napoleon (r. 1804-15)* of France promised to help Persia to recover its lost territory in the Caucasus in 1807.

On the suasin of England and France, Shah Fath Ali (r. 1797-1834) of Persia and Mahmud II (r. 1808-39) of Turkey proclaimed war against Russia in 1804 and 1808 respectively. The Persian army fought its first battle with the Russian army near Yerevan in Armenia and suffered defeat. France again sided with Persia on the termination of the Russo-French treaty of peace and alliance signed at Tilsit on the left bank of the Neman River on 7 July 1807after differences between Aleksandr (r. 1801-25) and Napoleon in 1812. Napoleon even invaded Russia and captured Moscow in September 1812. He suffered defeat in Paris under the army of Tsar Aleksandr in 1814. Persia and Russia signed their peace treaty at Gulistan, a village in Karabagh, on 12 October 1813. It imposed an indemnity of five million tumans on Persia, ceded to Russia all the Persian territory between the Caucasus and the Caspian and confirmed all the acquisitions of Russia, south of the Caucasus. There was no ratification of the Perso-Russian treaty until 1816. Even then, certain vague clauses of the treaty, especially with respect to the Perso-Russian frontiers, gave rise to diplomatic tussle and ill-feeling between Persia and Russia. That again led to war between them in August 1826.

* Napoleon took the title *Emperor* in 1804.

Initially, the Russian forces faced several reverses. Eventually, Persia used for peace. By the peace treaty, along with the commercial treaty, which Persia and Russia signed at Turkmanchai, a village south of Tabriz, on 22 February 1828, Persia further lost territory in Armenia and Azerbayjan. The Russian border moved south through the Caucasus to the Aras River. The treaty also imposed on Persia a payment of twenty million roubles as indemnification for the expenses of the campaign. The commercial treaty, separate from the political treaty but signed simultaneously with it, established consular jurisdiction and extra-territorial privileges for Russia in Persia. The political treaty began permanent involvement of Russia in Persia, and further east. It remained valid up to the end of the Tsarist regime in 1917. Aleksandr Sergeyevich Griboyedov (and his entire staff but one), who negotiated it, while overseeing it as the Russian minister at Tehran fell on 30 January 1829 to a mob, which burst into the legation building and destroyed and looted it. Shah Fath Ali apologized to Tsar Nikolai (r. 1825-55) on 11 February 1829.

By the Russo-Persian treaty of 1828 the sovereignty of the Caspian Sea passed to Russia : no ships of war, except Russian, on the Caspian Sea. So much so that the Caspian Sea became an exclusively Russian Sea. The treaty not only denied Persia the right to keep vessels of war in the Caspian but also forbade it to trade under its own flag from its own shores. On the plea of protecting Persian trade as well as Russian trade routes to Central Asia from the Turkmen pirates, the Russians started to construct fortresses on the eastern shore of the Caspian in 1838. With the authorization of Shah Fath Ali, they constructed a naval arsenal on the island Ashoor-ada at the mouth of the Bay of Astarabad.

The Russian government vigorously pursued subtle diplomacy towards Bukhara and Khiva from 1836 to 1842. It sent Colonel Butenev, along with Khanikov* and Lehman to Bukhara and Nikivorov to Khiva in 1841. Colonel Danilevski concluded a treaty with Khan Allahkuli, the Khan of Khiva, for the first time in 1841, providing for the cessation of slave trade and for restraining the Karakalpaks and Turkmens from inroads into Russian territory and molestation of Russian subjects. General V.A. Perovsky, Governor of Orenburg, marched an expeditionary force against Khiva from the Emba River across the Dasht-i Kipchak and the Ust-Urt deserts, between the Aral and Caspian Seas in mid-winter in 1839-40. The Russian government arrested all the Uzbek merchants resident at Orenburg and Astrakhan. The expedition failed from the severity of the season and scarcity of fodder.

Before dispatching another expedition against Khiva in the spring of 1873, the Russians occupied Krasnovodsk. They built its port and fortress in 1869. They established a military post at Chikishlar, near the mouth of the Atrek River, in 1871. The 1873-expedition against Khiva eventually led the Russians to the Marv oasis.

General Mikhail Dmitriavich Skobelev**, however, could not subdue the Tekkes, the largest and most powerful of the Turkmen tribes of the Akkal oasis between the Kopet Dagh range and the Karakum Desert before 1881. His forces first suffered defeat at the Dengil Tepe (also known as Geok Tepe) fortress on 12 January, 1881, 1 but took it on 24 February 1881. They had

* Baron de Bade translated in English Khanikov's previous Russian work on Bukhara (1841) under the title *Bukhara : its Amir and its people,* London, 1845.

** General Skobelev campaigned in the Turkmen region from 1877 to 1886.

Ashkabad between ancient Anau and Nisa on 15 January 1881. The Russian government absorbed the entire Turkmen territory into its Turkestan. It transferred its military base for Central Asia from Orenburg to the eastern shore of the Caspian Sea.

The governments of Persia and Russia settled their common boundary between Persian Khurasan and Russian Turkmenia by signing a convention on 21 December 1881. The subjection of the Turkmen tribes led to an improvement in the situation in West Central Asia. Shah Nasreddin (r. 1848-96) of Persia considered the advance of Russia favourably because of the relief it provided to the people of Khurasan from Turkmen brigandage and terror, and law and order on the Khurasan-Turkmen frontier, especially the disastrous blow the Turmens had given to the Persian army at Marv in 1860. Mirza Reza shot dead, by pistol, Shah Nasreddin on 1 May 1896.

The relations, which Russia established with Persia, brought the interests of Britain (based in India) and Russia in contact for the first time. The British government feared the advance of Russia towards Afghanistan and India. According to it, the Persian-Russian treaty of 1828 transformed the defence of India from a military to a political issue, from the fear of the advance of Russia towards India to the fear of the invasion of Russia on India. From the point of view of defence, Herat had always been strategically important to India from the time of Chandragupta (r. 324-298 BC) of the Maurya dynasty to the time of the Mughals, and so on. The Achaemini empire had extended up to the Indus River. That is also why Alexander the Great had marched into India.

The British government interpreted Persian-Russian treaty of 1828 to entitle the Russian government to post a consul at Herat, the gate to and the outwork, the bulwork of British India, in the event of its capture by Persia. It is notable that, in view of the Anglo-Russian alliance of August 1812 in the context of the Anglo-French rivalry, British officials had looked with favour on Russian advance in the Caucasus.

The siege of Herat by Shah Muhammad (r.1835-48), who had succeeded his grandfather Shah Fath Ali, in 1838, alarmed the British government. The British government suspected that the Russian government had instigated the Persian siege of Herat. Over this, Lord George Eden Auckland, Governor-General of British India from 1836 to 1842, went to war with Afghanistan, the First Anglo-Afghan War of 1838-42. It had first encouraged Shah Fath Ali of Persia to send troops to Herat as a counterpoise to the designs of Zaman Shah of Afghanistan on India in the beginning of the nineteenth century. Later, the British strategy had been to close the invasion routes into India, and take Kandahar and Herat. Persia raised its siege of Herat on 23 June 1838.

The British government obtained the same rights in Persia, as the Russian government, by the Anglo-Persian treaty of commerce signed at Tehran on 28 October 1841. However, owing to certain perceptions of the Anglo-Persian policy in the 1840-50s, their mutual relations deteriorated. Persian troops occupied Herat in October 1856. The British government went to war with Persia on 4 December 1856. The Persian government undertook to evacuate Herat under the terms of their treaty signed in Paris on 4 March 1857. The Afghan army captured it at the end of May 1863. Amir Dost Muhammad (r. 1834-63) absorbed it, before his death in Herat in June 1863, into Afghanistan as the consequence of the Anglo-Afghan agreement of 27 January 1857 and the Anglo-Afghan treaty of 30 March 1857, both signed in Peshawar.

Both Britain and Russia had no direct frontier with Afghanistan before the 1850s. But both advanced towards it, the British moving north from Panjab and Sindh and the Russians moving south from the Syr Darya, each feeling annoyed at the other getting in its way. Hence the Anglo-Russian struggle, the great game in Central Asia. The work of the English agents such as Alexander Burnes, Bailie Fraser, William Moorcroft, and others at the courts of Bukhara, Khiva and Kokand and the First Anglo-Afghan War led to the appearance of the Russian agents there.

The British government believed the aim of Russian advance was to take Afghanistan. Afghanistan, by virtue of its location, was vital to any plan for the defence of British India. The Russian government, feared that Afghanistan under British control and/or influence might become a disturbing factor Central Asia. Lord George William Frederick Claredon, the Secretary of State of Britain, and Prince Mikhail Gorchakov, the Foreign Minister of Russia, discussed the status of Afghanistan and reached an understanding on 31 January 1873 to recognize the Amu Darya as the border between Afghanistan and Bukhara. The British and Russian governments signed an agreement in London on 10 September 1885 to demarcate the Afghanistan-Bukhara boundary from the Heri Rud* in the west to the Amu Darya in the east.

Thus Afghanistan, which had won freedom from the Mughal and Persian imperialisms in 1747, inadvertantly became involved in the politics of the expanding British and Russian empires. Internal instability and Anglo-Russian struggle for primacy in Central Asia forced upon it the status of a protectorate. The Anglo-Afghan peace treaty, concluded at

---

* *Rud* is Persian for "river".

Gandamak in Afghanistan on 26 May 1879, as the consequence of the Second Anglo-Afghan War of 1878-80, established British protectorate over Afghanistan, depriving it the right to conduct its own foreign relations. The Anglo-Afghan treaty of 1879 also ceded to the British government the Khaybar Pass and the frontier areas of Kurram, Pishin and Sibi in Baluchistan. The British government jealously guarded its right to control Afghanistan against influence from other powers, especially Russia, thereby imposing a heavy price for its pledge of non-interference in the internal affairs of Afghanistan.

On 29 March 1885, after General Alikhanov, a Tatar Muslim from the North Caucasus, occupied Panjdeh, the Russian government claimed the Zulfikar Pass between Herat and Panjdeh as within the sphere which had come under it after its subjugation of the Turkmen tribes of the Marv oasis. The British government, which considered Panjdeh as part of Afghanistan, resented it. It had pledged, vide the Anglo-Afghan treaty of 1879, to safeguard the integrity of Afghanistan. Under no circumstance, it could tolerate any encroachment on it. There was Russian war hysteria in England and an Anglo-Russian War seemed imminent. Amir Abdur Rahman (r. 1881-1901) of Afghanistan was not sure, in his discussion with Lord Dufferin at Rawalpindi on 31 March 1885, if Panjdeh belonged to Afghanistan. The Anglo-Russian boundary protocol of 1887 assigned Panjdeh to Russia and the Zulfikar Pass to Afghanistan, thereby ending the crisis.

The delimitation of the Afghanistan-Bukhara boundary facilitated the travel of Western scholars and men of adventure in Central Asia. According to archaeological discoveries and researches (Raphael Pumpelley, Washington, DC, 1904), the civilizations of ancient Central Asia were cosmopolitan moulded by the impression of Iranian, Indian and Chinese influence on the local genius.

The Anglo-Russian boundary commission, set up vide the Anglo-Russian agreement signed in London on 11 March 1895, demarcated the Afghan-Russian boundary in the Pamir region from Lake Sarikol to Tagdumbash assigning a portion of Darvaz, where the Ab-i Panj (Panj River) bends to the north at Ishkashim, to Afghanistan and Ishkashim, Shugnan and Rushan to Russia. They had tenuously been connected with the Emirate of Bukhara. The Russian government made Ishkashim, Shugnan and Rushan over to Bukhara. The boundary commission established the Vakhan Corridor between the British and Russia empires, thereby separating the British and Russian territories in the Pamir region.

The strategic implications of a Russian wedge between Afghanistan and China were too obvious to the British government. London, therefore, proceeded to conclude an agreement with Petersburg to assign Vakhan to Afghanistan. The Afghan-Russian military collision at Somatash along the Ab-i Panj on 12 July 1892, in which the Afghans had been wiped out, had strained relations between Afghanistan and Russia, and Amir Adbur Rahman had been reluctant to take Vakhan. The British offer of an annual subsidy of Rs 1,00,000 to Amir Abdur Rahman was perhaps irresistible. Vakhan had been a small hereditary principality up to 1877 when it passed under the rule of the Emir of Bukhara.

The rise of Germany and Japan from 1895 onwards, especially the defeat of Russia by Japan in 1904, led the British and Russian governments to agree to settle their spheres of influence principally in Persia and signed a convention in St. Petersburg on 31 August 1907 to this effect. The British government undertook not to annex or occupy Afghanistan and the Russian government renounced direct contact with Afghanistan. Russia also agreed to regard Tibet as a neutral zone. Thus the negotiations, which the British and Russian governments had begun with the aim of creating a buffer state of Afghanistan, ended up by the carving out of their spheres of influence. It may be noted that the British and Russian governments did not consult the Persian government.

Before the Anglo-Russian convention of 1907, British and Russian authorities had spared no effort and/or means to create trouble for each other. The British authorities had sent their agents to Bukhara to incite its mullas against the Tsarist regime in Turkestan, and the Russian authorities had sent theirs to India to incite the Muslims against the Hindus. The convention of 1907 ended this. It ended more—the Anglo-Russian contest in central and West Asia.

The status of West Central Asia after conquest by Russia had been that of a colony with the administrative structure of the governorate general. The government of Tsar Aleksandr II (*b.* 1818; *r.* 1855-81) first discussed the administration of its part of West Central Asia in 1865. The *ukase* of 23 July 1867 separated Turkestan from the jurisdiction of Orenburg, and appointed General K.P. von Kaufman its first governor-general or general governor as styled by the Russians. The conquest of the Khanate of Kokand by General Kaufman in 1876 completed the subjugation of West Central Asia to Russia. The governorate general comprised the *oblasts*/ provinces of Syr Darya, Samarkand*, Fargana and Semirech'ye**, It restored the Sultan Bent dam in the autumn of 1890. The prosperity of the Marv oasis had been due as much on it as on the function of the caravan routes from Afghanistan, Bukhara, Khiva and Persia. It included the Oblast of Transcaspia in 1898. Until then, the Oblast of Transcaspia had been in the governorate general of the Caucasus formed on 10 May 1874, with its headquarters at Krasnovodsk. The administrative structure of Russian Turkestan underwent several changes up to the end of the Tsarist regime in 1917. There had been several attempts to reform it such as the investigation of Count Konstantinovich Pahlen in 1908-1909.

The Russian conquest of West Central Asia had been piece meal. Political considerations had motivated the Russian advance, and expansion. Nevertheless, the Russian administration brought about many changes in the life of its people. It brought a measure of prosperity without greatly disrupting the traditional way of life and values. It abolished slavery in Central Asia. It constructed railways—the Trans-Caspian Railway and the Orenburg Tashkent Railway, and so on. The construction of railways played an important part in the economic and social life of West Central Asia. Railway workers from as far as Sinkiang in China took active part in the revolution of 1917. However, apart from the Sart people, the Tajiks and Uzbeks, it did not induce the Kazaks, Kirgizes and Turkmens to exchange nomad, pastoral life for sedentary, agricultural life.

---

* Zeravshan Oblast up to 1886.

** Russian for the Turki *Jeti Su*, "Seven Rivers", that is the region of several parallel small rivers, such as Aksu, Chu, Sokuluk, etc, flowing north-west into Lake Balkash.

There were several revolts against the Tsarist rule in West Central Asia in the 18th and 19th centuries, such as the revolts of Batir* Srim of the Little Kazak Division in 1787. Khan Kenesari Kasimov (r. 1837-48), a grandson of Ablai Khan (1711-81) of the Orta Juz (Middle Kazak Division), revolted against the abolition of the Khanate. The Russian colonists took land away from grazing in the Kazak steppes. Kenesari Kasimov led the resistance against the land limitation in 1838. He asked the northern Kirgizes of the Ala Tau mountains, and the Khanate of Kokand to join him against the Tsarist regime. The Kirgiz *manaps*, clan chiefs, who had long been under the influence of the Khans of Kokand and who had established relations with the Russian administration, rejected his suggestion. Instead, they incited their people to raid the Kazak *auls*/villages. Kenesari Kasimov held a meeting of the chiefs of the Ulu Juz (Great Kazak Division), which decided to punish the Kirgiz manaps. The war against the Kirgizes ended in his defeat in 1841. In one of the battles, the Kirgizes captured him and killed him.

The *polozheniya*/ regulations of 1868 led to the revolt of the sultans, mullas and clan chiefs of the Kazaks, who stood to lose power, and privileges. After its suppression by the Russian army in mid-1869, large numbers of the Kazaks moved to the Ust'-Urt plateau, the Mugojar mountains and the Khanate of Khiva. The leaders of the revolt appealed to Khan Muhammad Rahim (r. 1865-1910), the Khan of Khiva, for acceptance as his subjects. Their appeal was futile. A decree of 25 June 1916, ordering mobilization of Central Asian men aged nineteen to forty-three, who had been exempt from military service, for duties

---

* Literally hero from the Persian *bahadur,* i.e. nobleman, clan chief.

behind the war lines precipitated the revolt of 6 October 1916.

There also had been movements for independence from Russia. Enlightened Kazaks, who had the experience of participation in the uprising of 1916, organized the *Alash Orda* in Orenburg in March 1905 and set up a provisional government of Kazakstan.

Like Tsarist Russia, Soviet Russia also did not take West Central Asia one piece. A congress of the Soviets of Turkestan held in Tashkent on 1 May 1918 declared Turkestan the first autonomous Soviet republic, inclusive of the territory of the Kazak tribes, within the Russian Soviet Federative Socialist Republic (RSFSR). The RSFSR accepted it within its framework on 11 April 1921. The Khanate of Khiva, renamed Khorezm, its ancient name, became the Khorezm People's Socialist Republic on 30 April 1920. The Emirate of Bukhara became the Bukhara People's Socialist Republic on 20 September 1920. The Soviet government in Moscow recognized them as sovereign states. On 5 March 1923, in a conference held in Tashkent the Uzbeks of Bukhara and Khorezm proclaimed to unite with their fellow Uzbeks of the ASSR of Turkestan.

During the first years, the Soviet government suffered several reverses and setbacks such as the Basmachi counter-revolution and restlessness over land collectivization. Inspired by Turkish nationalists such as Enver Pasha (1881-1922), the Basmachis incited the people against Soviet Russia. The foreign interventionists also conducted intrigues there through Afghanistan, Persia and Turkey. To nip all this, Vladimir Ilych Lenin (1870-1924) concluded his first treaties of friendship with Afghanistan, Persia and Turkey respectively in Moscow on 20 February,

26 February and 16 March 1921. Later, the Soviet government also concluded with their governments treaties relating to the regulation and use of their common frontier rivers.

The Soviet government also set up a delimitation commission on 27 October 1924 to reorganize the Turkestan ASSR. It reorganized the Turkestan ASSR, inclusive of the republics of Bukhara and Khorezm and the territories of the Kazaks, into the Uzbek Soviet Socialist Republic and the Kazak, Kirghiz, Tadzhik and Turkmen Autonomous Soviet Socialist Republics. The delimitation commission kept the southern parts of West Siberia with Kazakhstan. It also created autonomous regions and autonomous areas for the numerous ethnic groups. It created in Kazakhstan the autonomous district of Semirech'ye. The Hans, Dungans, Manchus, Turks, Slavs (Russians, Ukrainians), Germans live in Semirech'ye. It assigned the towns of Chimkent and Osh, mainly Uzbek, to Kazakhstan and Kirghizstan respectively. It assigned the Fargana Valley to Uzbekistan, Tadzhikistan and Kirghizstan. A part of Khorezm and the entire territory of the Turkmen tribes formed Turkmenistan.

Why did the delimitation commission of 1924 separate the Kazak territory from Central Asia? According to any definition of Central Asia, Kazakstan is part of West Central Asia. The Soviet authorities, it seems, had intended to colonize it separately. Although the delimitation commission divided West Central Asia into ethnic units, emphasizing differences in language and territory, political considerations were the main determinants. Be that as it may, the republics of Soviet Central Asia and Kazakhstan were fully sovereign by the mid-1930s.

The seat of the Uzbek SSR, was first at Samarkand. It moved to Tashkent in 1930. Uzbekistan joined the

USSR on 27 October 1924. Karakalpakistan, the land of the "black cap" Nogai Tatar tribe, so-called from their headgear, was first part of the Autonomous Soviet Republic of Kazakhstan. It became an autonomous oblast (region) in 1932, and affiliated to the RSFSR. It became part of the Uzbek SSR, and its autonomous oblast in 1936. Its administrative centre was first at Tortkul'/Aleksandrosk and at Nukus since 1939. Traditionally, the Karakalpaks have been semi rather than fully nomadic. The seat of Kazakh ASSR, created on 26 August 1920, was first at Orenburg in the RSFSR. Then it moved to Ak Mesjet, renamed Kizil Orda. The Turkmen ASSR became full Soviet Socialist Republic on 14 February 1925. The Tadzhik ASSR created, along with Gorno Badakshan (Highland, Mountainous Badakshan) Autonomous Oblast with its administrative centre at Khorog, on 15 March 1925, became full SSR and separated from Uzbekistan on 10 November 1929. Perhaps the delimitation commission so named Gorno Badakshan to distinguish it from the Badakshan of Afghanistan.

Gorno Badakshan (Darvaz, Rushan and Shugnan) in South Tajikistan is the primeval land of the Tajiks, the most ancient people of Central Asia speaking various ancient Iranian dialects. Whereas the Tajiks of the Republic are Sunni Muslims, the Tajiks of Gorno Badakshan are Shii Muslims of the Isma'ili Sect. The Gorno Badakshan Autonomous Region constituted more than half the area of the Tadzhik Soviet Socialist Republic.

The Soviet government created the Kazakh and Kirghiz Autonomous Soviet Socialist Republics on 26 October 1920. They became Soviet Socialist Republics and joined the USSR on 5 December 1936. The small town of Pishkak, Frunze since 1926, became the capital of Kirghizstan.

The Soviet constitution separated the Church and State, and provided freedom of religion. But the anti-religious propaganda tried to eliminate religion from Soviet life. The Soviet government closed religious places and schools, proscribed religious books such as the Bible and the Kura'n. It spared no effort, and means, to encourage atheism. During the Second World War (1939-45), however, it pursued a soft policy towards all religions in the USSR. In 1942, Josep Stalin (1879-1953) made a concordat with the prominent Tatar Mufti Abdurrahman Rasulev, giving Soviet Muslims a central religious organization with offices at Ufa, Mahhak Kala, Baku and Tashkent. Soviet Muslims responded by extending full cooperation in the war effort. An All Union Congress of Soviet Muslims held at Ufa, the capital of the Bashkir ASSR of the RSFSR, in June 1942 called upon Muslims everywhere to help defeat Nazism.

Towards the end of the 1980s, the Soviet government returned to the Spiritual Board for Muslims of Central Asia and Kazakhstan (DUMSAK). a number of old mosques such as the Kura'n Mosque in Bukhara and the Mausoleum and Mosque of Bahaettin Nakshband (1318-89), the great saint of Turkistan, in the suburbs of Samarkand. It also opened the tomb of Abu Muhammad, a native of the town of Termiz and the author of one of the six authentic books on the *hadis*/tradition, containing traditions from and about Prophet Muhammad and his companions. The *al-Jami al-Sahih* of Muhammad al-Bukhari (809/10-70), the corpus of traditions, is one of *the* most important sections in the collection of the *hadis*. Although the Muslims were quite aware of Moscow's motivation, they welcomed these concessions of expediency.

The Soviet government's language authorities changed the scripts of the Turkic languages of West Central Asia from Arabo-Persian first to Latin and then Cyrillic in 1924. Soviet scholars, who introduced alphabets based on modified Cyrillic alphabets, said that the Arabo-Persian script was impracticable in the case of the phonetic peculiarities of a number of Turkic languages (Uzbek, Turkmen, Kazak and Kirgiz) and its syntax and grammar unsuitable to those languages. Perhaps correct cyrillically, this distorted important names such as Ashkhabad for Ashkabad, Bakhouttin for Bahaettin, Mukhamedov for Muhammad, Tadzhik for Tajik, etc. The Russian custom of adding "ev"/"eva", "yev"/"yeva" to the last names of Muslim men and women also metamorphosed their names.

The Turkish linguistics had a long tradition in pre-revolutionary Russia. Many academic savants such as V.V. Radlov (1837-1918) and V.V. Barthold (1869-1930) had distinguished themselves as eminent Turkologists in the Tsarist period. But it was the Soviet authorities which made Russian the *lingua franca* in West Central Asia as elsewhere. The policy of linguistic unification there, however, always troubled the Soviet authorities.

Up to 1924, the Kazaks, Kirgizes, Tajiks and Turkmens had no scripts of their own. The literate Kazaks, Kirgizes and Turkmens used the Arabo-Persian script. The works of Abu Rayhan al-Biruni (972-1048/50), Abu Ali Ibn Sina (980-1035)—the great minds of Central Asia—and others such as Ali Shir Nava'i (1440-1502) were in this script. The literate Tajiks imbued themselves with the classics of Abu'l Hasan Rudaki (884-958), Abu'l Kasim Nureddin Firdusi (934-1020/25), Umar Khayyam (1022-1123), Mushrifeddin Muslih Sa'di (*c.* 1213/19-92), Amir Khusru Dehlavi (1213-1325). Muhammad Shamseddin Hafiz (1370-89), Abdel Rehman Jami (1441-92),

There was much development in West Central Asia in the Soviet period. The Soviet government developed agriculture, industry, communications, and so on. By developing agriculture, industry and communication, it transformed the land of nomads and herdsmen. Above all, it abolished illiteracy in West Central Asia, and raised the level of literacy there. Thus it changed the lifestyle and raised the standard of life of the people of Central Asia.

6

FLEDGLING STATES

Except for ethnical agitation in West Central Asia from 1986 to 1990 such as the riots in Alma Ata in December 1986 in protest against the appointment of Gennadii Kolbin (a Chuvash Russian) as the first secretary of the Communist Party of Kazakhstan in place of Dinmukhamed Kunaev on 17 December 1986, in Ashkhabad and Nebitdag in TurKmenistan in May 1989, in Dushanbe in Tadzhikistan on 11 February 1990, and so on, no political struggle in Soviet Central Asia and Kazakhstan for independence from the Union of Soviet Socialist Republics (USSR) had surfaced. The soveign republics of Soviet Central Asia and Kazakhstan created under the Soviet policy of nationalities in 1924 and 1936, like the other republics of the erstwhile USSR, declared their separation from the Soviet Union after the *coup d'etat* of 20 August 1991 against President Mikhail S. Gorbachev. Uzbekistan was the first to join the USSR on 27 October 1927 and the first to leave it on 31 August 1991. Kazakhstan was the last to join it on 5 December 1936 and the last to leave it on 16 December 1991.

On the dissolution of the Soviet Union, the Russian Soviet Federative Socialist Republic (RSFSR) and Belorussia (Belarus since then) declared to form the Commonwealth of Independent States (CIS) in Minsk, the capital of Belorussia, on 8 December 1991. The republics of West Central Asia declared in Ashkhabad, the capital of Turkmenistan, to adhere to the Minsk declaration on 13 December 1991 and joined the CIS in Alma Ata on 21 December. Turkmenistan attended the CIS meetings only as an observer in the beginning. The Alma Ata declaration formally put and end to the Soviet Union, founded in Moscow on 30 December 1922. The republics of West Central Asia committed themselves to the treaties signed by the erstwhile USSR.

The governments of the States of West Central Asia retained the Soviet institutions and infrastructures, but indigenized or reformed them. They changed the names and spellings of their republics, cities, streets and public places. Alma Ata, the capital of Kazakhstan, became Almati; Frunze, the capital of Kirghizstan, became Bishkek; Ashkhabad, the capital of Turkmenistan, became Ashgabat. Krasnovodsk, the only sea port of Turkmenistan, became Turkmenbashi. They removed the statues of Marx and Engels and Lenin and Stalin from public places. The Brezhnev Square in Alma Ata became the Republic Square; the Lenin Boulevard in Samarkand (Uzbekistan) became the Timur Boulevard. The Government of Uzbekistan built a majestic monument to Timur in the square of his name in Tashkent. The Uzbek Government has also constructed a museum of Amir Timur and Timuri dynasty in Tashkent. The Uzbeks now look on Amir Timur as the most heroic of Central Asia. All this has been a part of the Uzbek attempt to recreate a heroic history of Uzbekistan. The Government of Tajikistan named a street in Dushanbe. Isma'il Saman after the founder of the first ever Tajik dynasty in West Central Asia. Changes in the names of villages, towns and districts have been most in Kirgizstan.

The heads of state of the republics of West Central Asia at their meeting in Tashkent on 5 January 1993 changed the nomenclature of the region from Central Asia and Kazakhstan to Central Asia. The governments of the republics designed their own constitutions, anthems and flags. They changed to their own currencies, developed their custom posts,establi-shed their diplomatic missions abroad, and so on. The Presidents of Kazakstan, Kirgizstan and Uzbekistan at their meeting in Bishkek on 10 January this year signed an accord of eternal friendship among their brother nations.

Kazakstan

Kazakstan, the largest of the countries of West Central Asia between the Altai and Tianshan ranges in the east and the Aral and Caspian Seas in the west, borders Russia, Mongolia, China, Kirgizstan and Uzbekistan. The Kazaks also spread in Uzbekistan, Kirgizstan, Mongolia and Russia and in the Altai district of the Xinjiang Uigur Autonomous Region cf the People's Republic of China (PRC).

The Kazaks were the first Central Asian tribe, which Russia subdued in the 1730s and 1740s. For generations they had fought the Bsshkirs, a Finno Ugrian people inhabiting the region astride the south side of the Ural range, and the Tatars in their (Kazak) Orenburg territory. They are a minority in their own native land now : the Slavs (Russians, Ukrainians) are the majority community there. The Kazak leaders, in order to establish numerical equation with the Slavs, have called, unofficially of course, for the return of all Kazaks, who had fled their native land after the Russian revolution.

After the dissolution of the Soviet Union, Kazakstan was the first country of West Central Asia to sign an agreement with Russia in Moscow on 26 May 1992, calling for a single security zone between the two countries to be defended jointly, and for the common use of the Baikanor Cosmodrome, etc. In January 1995, Kazakstan and Russia agreed to unite their armed forces.

Uzbekistan

Uzbekistan, the most central of the countries of West Central Asia, borders Kazakstan, Kirgizstan, Tajikistan, Afghanistan and Turkeministan. The Uzbeks also live in all the other countries of West Central Asia, and in Afghanistan and China. Uzbekistan had a glorious past. Isma'il Saman founded its first historical dynasty (875-999). Khan Muhammad Shiban founded the Uzbek state in 1500. Except for the Buran Minar in Kirgizstan, and the tomb of Sultan Sanzar in Turkmenistan, most of the historical monuments of West Central Asia are in Uzbekistan.

After the disolution of the Soviet Union, Uzbekistan signed its first treaty of friendship with Russia at Moscow on 31 May 1992. At the signing ceremony, President Islam Karimov of Uzbekistan said that Uzbekistan understood the role of Russia in West Central Asia, and that "...without mutual cooperation with Russia, neither we nor our neighbours can overcome the present crisis." President Karimov has constantly emphasized the desirability of cooperation between Russia and the countries of West Central Asia. Kazakstan and Tajikistan have also developed, for different reasons of course, mutual relations with Russia. By the treaty on collective security signed in Tashkent on 15 May 1992, Russia holds the Amu Darya frontier of Tajikistan, Uzbekistan and Turkmenistan.

The Kazaks and Uzbaks descend from the Mongols and Turks. Their nobilities claim descent from Chingiz Khan. They were part of the Dasht-i Kipchak of Jochi, the eldest son of Chingiz Khan. The Kazaks founded their three Great, Middle and Little Divisions and converted to Islam. Originally the name Kazak and Uzbek were political, not ethnonyms. The Uzbeks derive their name from Uzbek Khan (r. 1312-42) of Dasht-i Kipchak.

Turkmenistan

Turkmenistan, a large country, borders Kazakstan, Uzbezistan, Afghanistan, Iran and the Caspian Sea. Like Uzbekistan, it is an antique land. Hyrcania (modern Gurgan) was the capital of Parthia. It was one of the sixteen localities successively created by Ormuzd. In its subsequent development, it included Khorezm, Khurasan and the western part of present-day Afghanistan. The writ of Cyrus (Kurush) the Great of Iran and Alexander the Great of Macedonia ran here. Parthia flourished between the first century BC and the beginning of the third century AD. In the beginning of the 2nd century AD, it was, along with China, India and Rome, one of the four great powers of the world. It extended up to the Eastern Mediterration. The Parthian civilization (c. BC 256-AD 226) thrived on this territory. The Parthians first built their capital at Nisa, near present-day Ashgabat. Marv (modern Mari) was a great stage on the ancient Silk Road. Islam first came to Marv in 651 AD. Khalifa/Caliph al-Ma'mun (r. 815-53), the son of Khalifa Ha'run al-Rashid (r. 786-809), entered Marv in 809.

The Turkmens are not the indigenous people of Turkmenistan : they are the descendants of the Iranians and Uigur Turks. They first appear in the Islamic sources in the 10th century. Their Turki is the most standard of all the Turkic languages of the Eastern and Western Turks. They also live in Kazakstan and Uzbekistan. The Persian-Russian convention of 1881and the Anglo-

Russian treaty of 1885 also placed them in Iran and Afghanistan.

The process of the transformation of the tribes of West Central Asia into nationalities had progressed sufficiently up to 1991, when they emerged as nations. Their transformation to full-fledged nations, however, was not quite complete then. Although they possessed the attributes of modern nations, they had not yet put their tribal past behind them. Also, they were not devoid of border and territorial disputes between them, and with their other neighbours such as China. There were parts of Siberia (Russia) in Kazakstan. The Kazaks claimed Orenburg. Turkmenistan voiced claim to the Mangishlak Peninsula on the north-east shore of the Caspian Sea. Uzbekistan claimed the Osh Oblast, the most agricultural part of Kirgizstan but Uzbek historically. The Karakalpaks wanted to separate from Uzbekistan. The states of West Central Asia had also faced the problems of refugees and migrants, and the related questions, Minorities spread all over West Central Asia. The Armenians, Baluchis and others live in Turkmenistan and the Jews, Koreans and others live in Uzbekistan. The Slavs live in all the countries of West Central Asia. What shape the inter-relations, political leanings and tribal loyalties of the post-independence states of West Central Asia ultimately take will determine their destinies.

The governments of the republics of West Central Asia, risen from the process of decolonization, accepted their colonial borders. Whether these borders were relevant or not, their redrawing can be dangerously volatile at any time. The work of the Delimitation Commission of 1924, though meant to divide the people of West Central Asia and break their unity then, has proved to be quite useful in retrospect. The leaders of the states of West Central Asia recognized, in a meeting in Bishkek on 23 April 1992, the "permanance" of their existing boundaries.

From north to south, Kazakstan and Turkmenistan are the large countries of West Central Asia. Kazakstan borders on China and Russia and Turkmenistan borders on Afghanistan and Iran. Kirgizstan and Tajikistan also border on China and Afghanistan. Hence their strategic importance. They are otherwise little countries. Kirgizstan is the smallest country of West Central Asia. Tajikistan is a solitary example unless the happening of the unforeseen.

Kazakstan and Turkmenistan are important in the context of China and Iran. The China-Kazakstan and Iran-Turkmenistan borders are long. Historically, Central Asia was of much concern to China and Iran. Both ancient China and Iran erected barriers and fortifications—China its Great Wall from the Gansu Province in the west to the Liaotung Peninsula in the east and Iran its Sadd-i Sikander, the wall of Alexander, north of the Kurgan River from the Caspian Sea in the west to the mountains in the east—against tribal depredations from the north. Instead of the former one Russian/Soviet border, China now has three borders with West Central Asia (that is Kazkstan, Kirgizstan and Tajikistan). There is no change in Iran's border with Turkmenistan. The Iran-Turkmenistan border, which had been closed after the Iranian Revolution of 1905-09, has been open since 1991, especially for border trade between them. Until 1680 there had been constant conflicts between the Persians and the Turkmens and the Uzbeks. The situation is different now : the people of West Central Asia, especially the Turkmens, look for exit passage, not for plunder, to the world through Iran. Krasnovodsk on the eastern shore of the Caspian Sea is Turkemenistan's only major port.

How do China and Iran feel now? Are Kazakstan and Turkmenistan of the same concern to them? The establishment of the diplomatic presences of China and Iran in West Central Asia shows their concern. As regards its over 3,500-mile long border with West Central Asia, the Government of the People's Republic of China first endorsed the documents, which it had signed with the government of the former USSR. On 26 April 1996, the Presidents of China and Russia, Kazakstan, Kirgizstan and Tajikistan signed in Shanghai a treaty relating to their 4,500-mile long border and aiming to strengthen confidence on their common borders. On 27 December 1996, their governments reached an accord in Beijing on reducing forces along those borders. On 24 April this year, the Presidents of China and Russia, Kazakstan, Kirgizstan and Tajikistan signed a treaty in Moscow to reduce troop levels on their borders. Iran has built up ties with the states of West Central Asia. It established an airlink between Mashhad and Dushanbe on 23 January 1992. It constructed a joint rail link between Mashhad and Sarakh in April-May 1996, providing Turkmenistan access to Bander Abbas in the Persian Gulf.

As between China, Iran and West Central Asia, the connection between India and West Central Asia is also historical. India's connection with Central Asia traces to the very dawn of civilization. But, except for a short sttip of Tajikistan in the Pamir region. India and the states of West Central Asia have no common borders. Yet India is their close neighbour, especially Tajikistan and Uzbekistan, for reasons of history and culture. India has full diplomatic presence in all of the states of West Central Asia. Its interests and concerns there are not like the interests and concerns of British or Mughal India. They are along different lines, i.e., along lines of equality and cooperation, not enmity or rivalry.

The destiny of the states of West Central Asia is unquestionably manifest. They are already members not only of the United Nations (UN) and its specialized agencies, Non-aligned Movement (NAM), Organization of Islamic Conference (OIC), Economic Cooperation Organization (ECO), and others. Uzbekistan first joined OIC as an observer. Their governments constantly explore ways and means of economic development through mutual cooperation (power, water, railways, outlets). They have done well so far. Except for Askar Akaev of Kirgizstan (he was then the head of the Academy of Science of his Republic), they were heads of the Communist Parties of their Republics, and most reluctant to break away from the Soviet state. They had no experience in self-government and world affairs. They have, however, frustrated thus far the game of power politics in their strategic region.

The states of West Central Asia have all that appertains to states. Their governments possess all the basic means, such as educational propaganda systems and so on, necessary to spread the idea of nationhood. Their natural resources—gas and oil and minerals and metals—are large. Their proper harnessing, and direction, can enable West Central Asia to resume its ancient title : "Garden of the East". Of course, this will greatly depend on the continuity and/or the increase or decrease of the pre-1991 developmental tempo, technological and economic, by the governments of the states of West Central Asia. And they still have to achieve viable political and social systems.

POSTFACE

Central Asia : An Outline History from the ancient time to the present reveals certain perspectives of the history of Central Asia. The sources of ancient China, India and Iran concerned with Central Asia, especially those of China, contain much material on the history of ancient Central Asia. Chinese sources are in the political context, Indian sources in the cultural context and Iranian sources in the Iran-Turan context. Accounts of medieval travels in Chinese and Arabic languages, valuable geographically and anthropologically, do not have much material on the history of medieval Central Asia. The accounts of travels of traders and envoys to or across Central Asia such as those of Ibn Battuta, the Polos and Ruy Gonzales de Clavijo contain material only on the non-historical aspects of Central Asia of their time. Sources of the history of modern Central Asia are scanty in no sense. The Manchu and Russian expansion in Central Asia as well as the British and Japanese thrusts there have been in the context of imperialism.

Cyrus of Iran and Alexandra of Macedon made crucial impact on the history of ancient Central Asia. But they were aliens from beyond its geographical bounds, and so was Chingiz Khan, the Mongol. For the ancient period, the great native Central Asians were Songtsen Gampo of Tibet and his dynasts and Isma'il Saman of Bukhara and his dynasts. The magnificent edifices of Songtsen Gampo and Isma'il Saman—the Potala in Lhasa and the Mausoleum in Bukhara—are among the great monuments of the ancient world.

The dynasts of Songtsen Gampo had the upper hand in East Central Asia and West China up to almost the first half of the 9th century AD. Bukhara was the "focus of splendour" during the period of the Samani dynasty. The tradition also continued during the later dynasties before the Mongol invasion.

Of the two natives, Temur of Samarkand and Zahiruddin Babur of Andijan, the latter fled Central Asia and sought fortune elsewhere. Temur almost but not quite united Central Asia in one sovereignty. Samarkand of the Timuri period excelled artistically, scientifically, and so on.

China, India and Iran had intimate connections with Central Asia in the ancient time. Russia is another close neighbour of Central Asia now. Contemporary Central Asia is strategically important to China, Iran and Russia. Will or will not the states of West Central Asia allow them or anyone of them to dominate, or gravitate towards, them? Owing to the circumstance of history, Russia is the prevailing power in West Central Asia. After Russia, China is the next prevailing power there. While China does not seem to be a contender for influence there now, Iran is. It has a cultural edge there.

The Farsi/Persian language of Iran was the language of culture, correspondence and literature, of the Khantes of Bukhara and Khiva up tc 1920. Cooperation between Iran and the states of West Central Asia will bring them further together now, of course, Iran has its limitations as well.

BIBLIOGRAPHY

Adshead, S.A.M., *Central Asia in world history,* London, 1993.

Allsen, Thomas, *Mongol Imperialism*, Berkeley : University of California Press, 1968.

Bosowrth, C.E., *The Ghaznavids : their empire in Afghanistan and Eastern Iran, 944-1040*, Edinburgh, 1963.

Dallin, D.J., *The Rise of Russia in Asia*, London, 1950.

Gibb, H.A.R., *The Travels of Ibn Battuta A.D. 1325-1354*, 3 vols., Cambridge, 1958-71.

Huntington, Ellsworth, *Pulse of Asia*, Boston, 1917.

Justi, F., *Central and Eastern Asia in Antiquity*, London, 1902.

Krader, Lawrence, *Peoples of Central Asia,* The Hague, 1963.

Kuno,Yeshushi, *Japanese expansion on the Asiatic continent.* 2 vols., Berkeley, 1937-45.

McGovern, William Montgomery, *The Early Empires of Central Asia : A study of the Scythians and the Huns and the part they played in World History*. Chapel Hill, N.C., University of North Carolina Press, 1939.

Parker, E.H., *A Thousand Years of the Tartars,* London: Kegan Paul, 1895.

Tarn, W.W., *The Greeks in Bactria and India,* Cambridge, 1938.

UNESCO, *History of Civilizations of Central Asia*, vol. I, Paris, 1992 ; eds. Dani, A.H. and V.M. Masson.

______, vol. II, Paris, 1994; ed. Janos Harmatta.

Wessels, C.J., *Early Jesuit Travellers in Central*

Asia, 1603-1721, The Haque : Martinus Nijhaff, 1924.

Yule, Henry, *Cathay and the Way Thither,* 2 vols., London : 6Hakluyt Society, 1866 ; ed. by Henri Cordier, 4 vols., 1913-1916.

INDEX

Abbasid Khilafat/Caliphate, 65
Abder Rashid, 71, 72
Abdul Latif, 106
Abdur Karim, 72
Abdur Rahman, Amir, 113
Abroka Pass, 52
Abu'l Malikshah, 100
Abu Ali al-Balami, 100
Abu Bakr, 70
Abu Bakr Duglat, 70
Abu Muhammad, 144
Abu Muslim, 65
Acharya Shantirakshita, 26, 27, 28
Adjaib al-Maqdur, 105
Afghanistan, 11, 14, 16, 109, 113, 114, 133, 143
Afghanistan-Bukhara boundary, 113, 114, 136
Afzal Khan, 113
Agitation, 147
Agvan Dorjiev, 50
Akbar the Great, 108
Aksakals, 79
Akshobhya, 23
Aktagliks, 73, 74
Alam Khan, 79
Alas Orda, 141
Aleksander, 130, 131, 153
Aleksandr II, Tsar, 81
Alexander the Great, 12, 16, 151
Alexandra of Macedon, 156
Al-Jami al-Sahih, 144
Alma Ata, 93, 126, 147
Alma Ata declaration, 148
Almora, 47
Almoti River, 126
Altan Khan, 37
Alti-Shahr, 14
Altyn Beshik, 17
Amanullah, Amir, 120
Amban, 43, 46, 75
Amir Abdur Rahman, 136
Amir am-mumin, 83
Amir Muhammad Yakub, 85, 86, 88
Amir Nasr II, 100
Amir, 98
Amitabha, 56
Amu Darya, 19, 98, 108, 110, 122
Amur River, 103
Anatolia, 104
Andijan, 56, 85, 86, 157
Anglo-Afghan agreement, 134
Anglo-Afghan treaty (1857, 1879), 135, 136
Anglo-Afghan war (1838-42, 1878-80), 135
Anglo-Chinese convention (1890), 49, 50, 51
Anglo-Chinese regulations (1893), 49, 50
Anglo-Chinese war (1838-42), 80
Anglo-Chinese-Tibetan Conference (1913-14), 51, 53
Anglo-Japanese alliance (1903), 49
Anglo-Kashgarhian treaty (1874), 83
Anglo-Persian treaty (1857), 134
Anglo-Russian agreement (1875), 81, 137
Anglo-Russian alliance (1812), 134, 135
Anglo-Russian boundary agreement (1885), 136
Anglo-Russian boundary protocal (1887), 136
Anglo-Russian convention (1907), 138

Anglo-Russian treaty, 151, 152
Anglo-Russian War, 136
Anglo-Tibetan convention (1904), 50
Arab Army, 65
Arab conquests in Central Asia, 97
Arab Khilafat, 95, 98
Arabic, language and script, 95, 156
Arabo-Persian script, 95, 145
Arslan Khan, 67
Arunachal Pradesh, 52
Arya river, 104
Ashoka, Emperor, 65
Ashvaghosa, 66
Ashkhabad, 147
Asia Department, *see* Aziaski Parikaz
Askar Akaey, 155
Astrakhan, Haji Tarkan, 124
Atalik Ghazi, 82
Atisha, Deepankara Srijnana, 25, 33
Atrek River, 132
Auckland, Lord George, 134
Auli Ata, 65
Aurangzeb, Prince, 110
Austria, 68
Autonomous Soviet-Republic of Turkestan, 118
Azam Khan,
Aziaski Parikaz, 115

Babar, Zahiruddin, 71, 107, 110, 157
Bactria, *see* Bakhtar
Badakshan Gorno, 143
Baghdad, 67
Baghdad Khilafat, 65, 101
Bahadur Khan Abu'l Gheni, 121
Bakhtar, 97
Kaku,144
Balti, Baltistan, 71
Baluchis, 152
Bander Abbas, 154
Barthold, V.V., 145
Basmachi Counter revolution, 141
Batir Srim, 140
Battle of Taraz. 65
Bedevlat, 82
Belsa, *see* Bhrikuti Devi
Bezak, A.P., 127
Bhola, 12
Bhrikuti Devi, Princess, 23, 24
Bhutan, 11, 12, 23, 43, 44
Bhutan-India-Tibet trijunction, 53
Bhutan-Tibet agreement (1730), 44
Bible, 144
Bishkek, 153
Black mountaineer, 72
Bodhipathapradeepa, 34
Bodhisattva, 28
Bolshevik Revolution, *see* Russian Revolution
Bon, 13
Brahmaputra River, 13
Britain, 21, 48
Brusha, *see* Gilgit
Buddha anniversary celebrations, 60
Buddha, 24, 48
Buddhism, 13, 20, 25, 27, 30, 32, 33, 35-36, 65, 66
Bugra Khan, Muhammad, 67, 68
Bukhara, 16, 19, 63, 78, 88, 156
Bukhara People's Socialist Republic (BPSR), 121, 123, 141
Bukhara Russian treaty, 115
Bukhara Sharif, 97, 110, 112, 116, 117, 129
Burma/Myanmar, 12, 69
Buryat Mongol(s)/Buriyatia, 50

Byzantine (Eastern Roman) Empire, 104

Calcutta, 44, 45, 49, 83
Caspian Sea, 11
Catherine the Great, 129
Ch'ang Ch'ien, 62, 63
Ch'ang-an, 26
Ch'iang tribes, 22, 23
Ch'ien Lung, Emperor, 43, 46, 55, 75
Ch'ing-shui, 27
Chagatai Khan, 72
Chait Singh Raja, 55
Chak Turk dynasty, 71
Chandra Shamsher, Maharaja, 50
Chandragupta, Emperor, 133
Chang Chhub Gyat, 33, 34
Changthang (*Byang thang*), 12
Chang Weipei, 50
Chengdu (Ch'engtu), 51
Chewang Araptan, 42
Chhewang Dondub, 42
Chhokyi Nyima Panchhen Lama, 55
Chhos, 33
Chhosi Shungdd, 39
Chhumbi Valley, 48, 50, 51
Chiang Kai-shek, 56, 92
Chiangchin, 76
China, 11, 21, 28, 29, 153, 154, 157
Chinese Revolution (1911, 1949), 52
Chinese Russian treaty, 125, 127
Chinese-Tibetan treaty, 58
Chingiz Khan, 35, 68, 69, 102, 103, 150, 156
Chokha gsum, 36
Chongjing/Chongking, 92
Chu (River), 19, 67, 99
Chun-ch'en, Shan-yu, 76
Chung Hou, 87
Chung Tsung, Emperor, 26, 98
Commonwealth of Independent States (CIS), 147
Communist Party of China (CPC), 91
Communist Party of the Soviet Union (CPSU), 91
Comolungmo (Mount Everest), 13
Cooch Behar, *see* Koch Bihar
Cornwallis, Lord Charles, 45
Crimea, 87
Curzon, Lord George Nathaniel, 49
Custom, 31
Cyrillic script, 145

Dalai Lama Thubten Gyasto, 48, 51
Dalai Lama, 32, 37, 39, 40, 61, 62, 64, 68, 70
Darjeeling, 49
Dasht-i Kipchak, 18, 124
De Facto Autonomy, 52
Dejong (Dendzong), 45, 46
Delek Namgyal, 40
Delimitation commission 142, 152
Depung Monastery, 42
Dharmapala, King, 27
Dharmashala, 60
Dibang river, 52
Divan-i Hikmat, 99
Diwan-l Lughat at-Turk, 95
Dolma, *see* Tara
Dost Muhammad, Amir, 111, 113, 134
Dub thab, see siddha
Duglat, 69
Dungan/Tungan '7, 86
Dunhuang/Tunhuang 26, 63
Durrani, Ahmad Shah, 109
Dushanbe, 154

East Central Asia, 11
East India Company (Calcutta), 44, 45, 55
Economic Cooperation Organization (ECO), 155
Edward VII, 51
Elizabeth, Empress, 80
Emba River, 76, 132
Emir Abdul Ahad, 116
Emir Abdullah Mumin, 127
Emir Aim, 120
Emir Hayder, 110
Emir Muzaffer, 115
Emir Muzaffereddin, 113
Emir Nasrullah, 110, 112
Emir Timur, 20
Engels, Friedrich, 148

Fa Hsian, 16
Faizullah Khoja, 119
Fatwah, 77
Fidai Khan, 40
First Anglo-Afghanistan War, 134, 135
First Anglo-Chinease War, 80
Fort William, 44
France, 48, 104
Fuch'ing, 43
Fyodor Ivanovich, Tsar, 108, 124

Galchas, 17
Galdan Khan, 41, 73
Ganga, 13
Gansu/Kansu 12
Garhwal, 32
Gelug Theocracy, 39
George Bogle, 44
Germany, 137
Gilgit, 23
Ghusi Khan, 38
Glimpses of High Politics, 115
Gonpa, 13
Gorbachev, Mikhail S., 147
Gorkha(s), 45, 46
Great Wall, 26, 153
Guchuk Khan, 69
Guge Monarchy, 32, 35
Gurgenj Urgench, 102
Guru Rinpochhe, 28
Gushi Khan, 38
Gyalpo Pandita, 38
Gyaltshen, Chang Chhub, 36
Gyalwai Domton, 55
Gyasa, *see* Wen-ch'eng
Gyurmi Namgyal, Prince, 43

Hadis tradition, 144
Hami/Komul, 88
Han dynasty, 62
Han(s), 15
Hari Chand, Diwan, 47
Hastings, Warren, 44
Hazrat-i-Turkistan, 104
Hazrat Afak/Apak, 73
Herat, *He (Ho)*, 13, 134
Heri Rud, 135
Himalaya, mountain range, 11
Hsi Yu, 11
Hsian-pei, 62
Hsiung-nu(s), 62, 64
Hsuan Tsiang, 16
Huang He (Ho), 25
Huang Mu-sung, 56
Humayun, Emperor, 71
Huna, *see* Hsiung-nu
Hungary, 68
Hunza, 94

Ibm Khaldun, 105
Ibn Battuta, 156
Ibrahim Khan, 40
Ibrahim Lodi, 71
Ibrahim Shah, 71
Ili River Valley, 15, 38, 41, 73
Iltaz Khan, 110
India-Burma-China trijunction, 53

India/Indian(s), 12, 40, 157
Indus River, *see* Sindh (Sindhu),
Iran/Persia, 11, 21, 153, 154, 157
Iran-Turan Context, 156
Iranian Revolution, 153
Iraq, 11, 21
Irtish River, 83
Islam, 18, 74, 75, 78
Islamic Association, 92
Isma'il Saman, 156
Isu Razi Pass, 53
Italian Jesuit, 58
Itil River, Middle Volga River, 76

Jadidism movement, 116
Jahangir 77, 80
Jalaleddin Mankabirmi, 103
Jambul, 65
Jammu, 47
Jammu and Kashmir, 94
Jammu-Tibet treaty (1842), 48
Jammu-Tibet war (1841–42), 48
Jampel Gyatso Dalai Lama, 44, 45
Japan, 20, 21, 25, 50, 137
Jerusalem, 100
Jew(s), 14
Jihad, 70, 77
Jilegu Gurkhan, 69
Jo Khang, 23, 24, 30
Jochi, eldest son of Chingiz Khan, 35, 68, 69
Juma '*Namaz*', 70
Junayt Khan, 122

K'ang Hsi, Emperor, 42, 44
Kabul, 40, 70, 91, 110, 113
Kadir Khan, 67
Kalimpong, 52
Kama River, 124, 125
Kamalasheela, 28
Kamareddin Tuglat, 69
Kandahar, 134
Kao-tus, 23
Kao Tsung, Emperor, 26
Karakhan Dynasty, 67, 99
Karma Tenchong, 38
Kashgarh, 63, 69, 70, 118
Kashgarhia, 14, 67, 76, 82
Kashgarhian-Russia agreement, 84
Kashmir, 24, 32, 40, 66, 71, 81
Kathmandu, 45
Katta tura, 79, 113
Kaufman, K.P. Von, 138
Kazakstan, 143, 149
Kenesary Kasionov, 140
Kesang Gyatso Dalai Lama, 44
Khagyur, 35
Khalifa Harun al-Rashid, 151
Khalifa Kaliph al-Ma'mun, 151
Khan Abdul-aziz, 108
Khan Abdullah II, 108
Khan Iman Kuli, 108
Khan Isfandiyar, 122
Khan Muhammad Amin, 112
Khan Mohammad Rahim, 122, 123
Khan Ubaydullah, 107
Khanates, 124
Khiva Khanate, 121
Khizr Khoja, 69
Khoja Advent, 72
Khoja Ahmad Kasani, 72
Khoja Khan, 74
Khoja Niyaz, 91
Kholan, 65, 66
Khorezon People's Socialist Republic (KPSR), 123, 141
Khorgos River, 17, 87
Khoshot Mongol(s), 42, 72
Khotan, 14, 15, 24, 25, 29
Khudayar Khan, 82
Khurasan, 68, 97
Khutba, 70
Khwarazm Shali, 102

Kilaochi, 82
Kipchak, 18
Kirgizes, 17, 18, 94, 95
Koch Bihar, 44
Kokand Khanate, 78, 111, 123
Kokonor region, 22, 38, 42
Kolesov's Red Guards, 119
Korea/Korean(s), 20, 21
Kuangwa, Emperor, 64
Kunlun, 15
Kublai Khan 13, 35, 36
Kudatku Bilik, 68
Kulja, 88
Kumarajeeva, 66
Kumbum Monastery, 42, 51
Kunal, Prince, 65
Kuomintang (KMT), 88
Kura'n, 128, 144
Kurilatai, 121
Kyide Nyimagon, 31

Ladakh, 11, 13, 32
Ladakh-Tibet border, 40, 48
Ladakh-Tibet treaty (1683), 48
Lahore, 135
Lake Balkash, 15
Lake Manassarovar, 40
Lake Mapham, 12
Lama Chhodub Gyasto, 45
Lama Phakpa, 35, 36
Lama Sonam Gyatso, 37
Lansdowne, Lord Charles Keith, 49
Lawrence, Lord John, 114
Lenin, V.I., 19, 48
Lhasa, 23, 24, 29, 30, 35, 40, 42
Lhasa-Nyarong War, 48
Ligdan Khan, 77
Li Kuang-li, 64
Lingua franca, 145
Little Bukhara, 88
Liu P'u-chen, 56
Livadia, 87
Lobsang Khan, 41, 42
Lobzang Dakpa, 35
Lobzang Gyatso, Dalai Lama, 32, 39, 40, 44, 51, 55
London, 135
Lord Dufferin, 136

MacMahon/MacMahon Line, 34, 53, 54
Magadha, 25, 27
Mahavyutpatti(s), 29
Mahmud al-Kashgarhi, 67
Maitreya, 23
Makka (*Mecca*), 129
Malazgird/Manzikert, 100
Manchu Ch'ing dynasty, 42 43, 50, 52
Manchu China, protectorate of, 43
Manchu Primary, 74
Manchu(s), 42
Manifesto, 118
Manjushri, Bodhisativa, 40
Manning, Thomas, 58
Mao Zedong, 58, 93
Marlowe, Christopher, 104
Marpa, 34
Marx, Karl, 148
Mashhad, 106, 118, 154
Maurya dynasty, 133
Mawarannahr, 103, 105
Mediterranean Sea, 63
Mesopotamia, 63, 116
Miller, A.Y., 117
Ming dynasty, 37, 39
Ming Ti, Emperor, 64, 66
Mir Alam, 109
Mir Hayder, 109
Mir Masum, 109
Mogolistan, 14, 69
Mongol imperialism, 12
Mongol Yuan dynasty, 64
Mongol(s), 35
Mongol-China, regency, 35-38

Mongolia/Mongolian People's Republic, 17, 93
Mongolian Buddhism, 35
Mongolian script, 36
Moravia, 68
Moscow, 91, 92, 122, 148
Moscow's motivation, 144
Mount Tise, 12
Mu-tsung, Emperor, 29
Muhammad al-Bukhari, 144
Muhammad Amin, 78
Muhammad Hayder Duglat, 18, 71
Muhammad Rahim, 140
Muhammad Yakub, 83, 84
Mukden, 39
Muslionan Kul, 112
Mussoorie, 61
Mustafa Chokaiev, 119
Muthi Tsenpo, 28
Muzaffereddin, 109, 113

Nadir Shah, 108, 121
Nalanda Vihara, 25, 27, 28
Napoleon, Emperor, 130
Naryn River, 19, 84
Nasrullah Khan, 78, 109
Nehru, Jawaharlal, 60
Nepal, 11, 12, 34, 45, 48, 49, 50
Nepal-Tibet Conflict, 45
Nepal-Tibet treaty (1856), 49
Nepal-Tibet War (1855-56), 46, 48
New Kadam Sect, 35
Ngawang Jigdak, 38
Non-Aligned Movement (NAM), 155
Nubra Valley, 70

Oasis Kingdoms, 64, 68
Oirat Mongol(s), 41
Okkalar, 79
Omar Khayyam, 101
Onon River, 17, 29
Opamed, *see* Amitabha
Opium War, *see* Anglo-Chinese War
Ordam Padshah, 67
Orenburg Tashkent Railway, 139
Orenburg, 126, 152
Organization of Islamic Conference (OIC), 155
Orkhon inscriptions/region, 16, 66
Orla Juz, 126
Osh Oblast, 152
Osung, 31
Oxyartes, Persian King of Bactria, 97

Pacific Ocean, 125
Padshah, 74
Pamir Valley, 19, 63
Pan Ch'ao, 64
Panchhen Lama, 44
Panjab, 47, 135
Penjikent, 99
People's Liberation Army (PLA), 92, 93
People's Republic of China (PRC), 12, 58, 59, 60, 93, 96, 149, 154
Persia, 68
Persian Revolution (1907), 130
Persian Russian Treaty, 133
Persian Russo treaty, 131
Persian, language and script, 131
Persian-Russian convention (1881), 132, 151
Peshawar, 134
Phola, Sonam Tobgye, 43
Poland, 68
Polos, 156
Polozhehiya, 140
Ponchhen, 36
Portugal, 20, 32

Potala, 55, 56
Pu-i, Emperor, 51
Purang, 32

Qadimi, 116
Qarakitai Dynasty, 68
Qinghai (Ch'inghai), 14, 88
Queen Nantshulma, 30
Queen Victoria, 83
Qutaiba, Ibn Muslim, 97, 98

Radlov, V.V., 145
Rahim Kuli, 111
Ranbir Singh, Maharaja, 83
Ranjeet Singh, Maharaja, 47
Rawalpindi, 136
Repachan, 29, 30
Republic of China (ROC), 53, 54
Republic of East Turkistan (RET), 90, 91, 92
Rinchhen Zangpo, 32
Rizakuli, son of Nadir Shah, 108
Roksane, 97
Roman Catholic Mission Strangers, 48
Roxsana, *see* Roksane
Russia, 11, 21, 50, 68
Russian-Ecclesiastical Mission, 128
Russian-Revolution(1917), 89, 116, 149
Russian-Soviet Federative Soviet Republic (RSFSR), 123, 141, 143, 147
Russo-Bukharan treaty (1868), 123
Russo-Japanese War (1904), 56
Russo-Khivan treaty (1849, 1873), 126
Russo-Persian treaty (1813, 1828), 127
Ruy Gonzales, 156

Sabit Damulla, 90
Safavi dynasty, 107
Sahi Bukhari (*al-Jami al-Sahi*), Saman dynasty, 16
Sahib Kiran, 103
Saljuk dynesty, 101
Samani dynesty, 99, 157
Samarkand, 20, 139, 157
Samye Monastery, 27
Sanskrit, language and script, 26
Sarbaz (infantry), 112
Second Anglo Afghanistan War, 136
Second World War, 144
Semiplatimk, 127
Senalek, 29
Shah, Fath Ali, 131
Shah Jahan, Emperor, 110
Shah, Muhammad, 134
Shah, Nasreddin, Emperor, 133
Shah, Prithvinarayan, 45, 55
Shah, Sultan Husayn, 128
Shah, Tahmasp II, 129
Shakabpa, W.D., 60
Shan-yu Chichu, 62
Shash, 98
Shejaral-al-Turk, 121
Sheng Sui-tsai, 91, 92
Sheng T'ai, 49
Shibak, *see* Shibani, Muhammad, 108
Shibani Dynasty, 108
Shia Muslim, 143
Shiwaling Monastry, 47
Shun Chih, Emperor, 39
Sian Fang, Emperor, 48
Siberia, 16, 69, 75
Sichuan/Szechwan, 12
Siddhas, 34
Sikkim, 46, 49
Silk Road, 63, 65
Simla (Shimla), 53
Sindh (Sindhu) River, 13, 81, 103, 133

Sinkiang (Hsinkiang), 14, 76, 89
Sino-Russian treaties (1689, 1737, 1851, 1860, 1864, 1879, 1881), 81, 88
Sino-Soviet agreement (1924), 89
Sino-Soviet conflict, 88
Sino-Soviet treaties (1937), 87
Sino-Tibetan agreement (1951), 59, 60
Sino-Tibetan boundary dispute, 54
Siyasatnama/ Siyar al-Muluk, 101
Skobelev, Mikhail Dmitriavich, 132
Slav(s),
Sogod, Kingdom, 97
Songtsen Gampo, 22, 24, 25
Soviet-Persian treaty (1921), 132
Soviet-Turkish treaty (1921), 117
St. Petersburg, 87, 122, 138
Stkkim (Sukhim), *see* Dejong,
Strasbourg, 61
Su-tsung, Emperor, 30
Sufi Saint-Ahmad, 99
Sultan Abdel, 83
Sultan Abu Sa'id Khan, 70
Sultan Itusayn Baykara, 106
Sultan Khizr, 104
Sultan Malik Shah, 101
Sultan Shah Rukh, 105, 106
Sun Yat-sen, 52
Sunni Muslim, 143
Sutsung, Emperor, 27
Syr Darya, 19
17-point agreement, 58

T'ang dynasty, 23
Ta-li (Dali), Kingdom, 31
Tadzhik Soviet-Socialist Republic, 143
Taglakhar, 47
Tahmasp and Tahmasp II, 107
Tajikistan, 11, 14, 17, 20, 21, 143
Talas river, 65
Tangut, *see* Ch'iang
Tangyur, 34, 35
Taotai, 89
Tara, 23
Tarikat, 86
Tarikh-i Rashidi, 18, 72
Tarim river,15
Tashi Tsen, 31
Tashkent, 82, 85, 127, 141, 142, 148
Tatar Mufti Abdurrahman Rasulev, 144
Tattva Sangraha, 28
Te-tsung, Emperor, 27
Teesta River, 49
Tehran, 134
Tenzing Coyastso, 58
Thide Tsuglen, 26
Thisang Detson, 26, 27, 28, 29
Tholing Gonpa, 32
Thonmi, 24, 25
Three Districts Revolution, 93
Tibat (*Tubat*), 12, 13, 15
Tibetan autonomy, 60
Timur Amir, 104, 105
Timur lang, 103
Timur Shah, 109
Tobol river, 75
Tokharika, 66
Tolui Khan, 35
Tongsa, 49
Topawei dynasty, 66
Trade Agencies in Tibet, 59
Tranchi (Uigurs), 77
Trans Caspion Railway, 139
Tsaidam, 12
Tsang po (g Tsang po) 13, 23, 36, 40
Tsangyang Gyatso, 41,
Tsar Aleksandr II, 114, 123, 138

Tsar Ivan IV, 108, 124, 125, 128
Tsar Nikolai II, 117, 127, 131
Tsar Peter, 128, 129
Tsheten Dorji, 38
Tshurphu Monastery, 38
Tu-fan, 12
Tuglak Temur, 69
Tugril, 100
Turkey, 91
Turki, language and script, 17, 68, 145
Turkish revolutions, 116
Turkistan, 16, 91, 100
Turkmen, 17
Turkman Autonomous Soviet Socialist Republics, 142
Turkmenistan, 11, 17, 151
Tzu Hsi, Dowager Empress, 51

Ubasa/Ubasi Khan, 76
Uch Bel Pass, 81
Udantapuri Vihara/Bihar-i Sharif, 27
Ufa, 144
Uigurs, 66
Ugyen Wangchhuk, Ponlop of Tongsa (Bhutan), 49
Ula (Chin Yishan) system, 37
Ulu Juz, 126
Ulug Beg, 105, 110
Umar Khayyam, 101, 110, 145
Union of Soviet Socialist Republics (USSR), 147
United States of America (USA), 144
Ural, range and river, 76
Urumtsi, 76, 94, 95
Uzbek Khan, 151
Uzbek Khanates, 106
Uzbekistan, 11, 17, 18, 147, 148, 149, 150

Vakhan, 137
Vali Khan Tura, 79, 80, 87
Varanasi, 55
Viharas (Monasteries), 13, 16
Vihara Sangha, 34
Vikramsila Vihara, 33, 34
Volga River, 55, 76, 124, 125
Volga-Ural region, 55

Wan Li, Emperor, 37
Washington, DC., 60 137
Wei River Valley, 66
Wen-ch'eng, Princess, 23, 24
Western Region, *see* Xi Yu
White mountaineer, 72
White Russian refugees, 89, 93
William Frederick Claredon, 135
World War, 54
Wu Chung-hsin, 56, 92
Wu Ti, Emperor, 62
Wumi T'ai, 44
Wun Sin-kong, Princess, 26

Xi Yu (*Hsi Yu*), 11
Xian, *see* Ch'ang-an
Xinjiang Uigar region, 62
Xingiang Uigar Autonomous Region (XUAR), 14, 62, 94, 95, 149
Xining (Hsining), 18
Xinjiang (Sinkiang), 11 14, 15, 16, 18, 62

Yakub Bey, 82
Yamgurchai, 124
Yangze (Yangtse), 13
Yao Ch'ang, Emperor, 66
Yarkand, 14, 15
Yarlung Monarchy, 23, 31
Yasa(*k*), 104
Yatung, 48, 58
Yehonala, *see* Tzu Hsi,
Yellow Temple, 51
Yenisei River, 17

Yeshi Od, 32, 33
Yonten Gyal-so, 41
Young Bukharan Party, 118, 119, 120, 121
Yuan Shi-kai, (President), 52
Yulduz river, 15
Yumten, 31
Yunnan, 12, 31, 44, 54
Yung Cheng, 43
Yung Drung, 13
Yung Lo, Emerpor, 104

Zafar Nama, 105
Zahiruddin Muhammad Babar, 20, 70
Zarafshan River, 19, 97, 103
Zhou-Enlai, 60
Zij-e Jadid-e Sultani-Zij-e Ulug Beg, 106
Zorawar Singh, 47
Zoroaster/Zorastrism, 16, 17
Zoroastrian, 98
Zulfikar Pass, 136
Zungar Mongol(s), 75
Zungaria, 14, 76